Proceedings of the 1974 Clinic
on Library Applications
of Data Processing:
Application of Minicomputers
to Library and Related Problems

Papers presented at the
1974 Clinic on Library Applications
of Data Processing, April 28–May 1, 1974

# APPLICATIONS OF MINICOMPUTERS
# TO LIBRARY AND RELATED PROBLEMS

Edited by
**F. WILFRID LANCASTER**

**University of Illinois**
**Graduate School of Library Science**
**Urbana-Champaign, Illinois**

© 1974 by the Board of Trustees of the University of Illinois

LC Card Number: 65-1841
ISBN: 0-87845-041-6
U.S. ISSN: 0069-4789

# ACRONYMS

| | |
|---|---|
| APL | A Programming Language |
| ARPA | Advanced Research Projects Agency |
| ASCII | American Standard Code for Information Interchange |
| ATS | Administrative Terminal System |
| BALLOTS | Bibliographic Automation of Large Library Operations using a Time-sharing System |
| BNB | British National Bibliography |
| BPI | Bits per Inch |
| BPS | Bits per Second |
| CDC | Control Data Corporation |
| CHASM | Chicago Access Support Module |
| CID | Centre for Information and Documentation (of the European communities) |
| CLSI | Computer Library Services, Inc. |
| COM | Computer Output Microfilm |
| CPS | Characters per Second |
| CPU | Central Processing Unit |
| CRT | Cathode Ray Tube |
| DCM | Data Communications Multiplexor |
| DEC | Digital Equipment Corporation |
| DMA | Direct Memory Access |
| EDP | Electronic Data Processing |
| ESRO | European Space Research Organization |
| FAC | File Access Channel |
| FLS | Faculty of Library Science (University of Toronto) |
| HASP | Houston Automatic Spooling Program |
| I/O | Input/Output |
| IOC | Input/Output Channel |
| IOCS | Input/Output Control System |
| IPS | Inches per Second |
| IR | Information Retrieval |
| Inspec | Information Service in Physics, Electrotechnology and Control |
| ISBN | International Standard Book Number |
| LC | Library of Congress |
| MARC | Machine-Readable Cataloging |
| MDS | Microform Data Systems, Inc. |
| MEDLINE | MEDLARS On-Line |
| Ns | Nanosecond |
| OEM | Original Equipment Manufacturer |

| | |
|---|---|
| OS | Operating System |
| OULCS | Ontario University Libraries Cooperative System |
| POS | Point of Sale |
| RECON | Remote Console |
| RIOT | Retrieval of Information by On-line Terminal |
| ROM | Read Only Memory |
| SDI | Selective Dissemination of Information |
| SILC | System for Interlibrary Loan Communications |
| TCU | Transmission Control Unit |
| TYMNET | Tymshare Network |
| UTCC | University of Toronto Computer Centre |
| UTLAS | University of Toronto Library Automation System |
| VS | Virtual Storage |

# TABLE OF CONTENTS

# INTRODUCTION

It is widely recognized that library automation is most likely to be economically justifiable through (a) the sharing of computer resources among a number of libraries, by networking or other cooperative arrangements, or (b) the use of minicomputers within the complete control of a single library. Cooperation in data processing was the subject of the clinic of 1973. It is fitting, therefore, that the other approach, the use of minicomputers, should have been the theme of the 1974 clinic, the proceedings of which appear in this volume.

These papers present a wide range of applications of minicomputers to library-related problems: circulation control, cataloging, education and training, information retrieval, acquisitions, serials control, and other technical processes. In some applications the minicomputer is a stand-alone unit, in others it is a "front end" device in a larger equipment configuration, and in the application discussed by Waite, the minicomputer is incorporated into an on-line terminal operating within a dispersed computing network. An important element in this clinic was the tutorial on minicomputers in libraries, presented by Divilbiss and Corey.

This clinic was attended by well over 100 representatives from all types of libraries. A formal evaluation, conducted by questionnaire, indicated that the clinic was received with enthusiasm by the majority of participants. The evaluation was also very useful in bringing out suggestions from the participants on topics for future clinics, as well as suggestions as to how the format of these meetings might be improved in the future.

F. WILFRID LANCASTER
*Editor*

*1*

J. L. DIVILBISS
Associate Professor
Graduate School of Library Science
University of Illinois
Urbana-Champaign

# A Hardware Tutorial

## A BRIEF HISTORY OF THE MINICOMPUTER

In a practical sense, the minicomputer age began in 1964 with the Digital Equipment Corporation's introduction of the PDP 8. Potential computer users who had been unable to afford a $500,000 machine found that for the then remarkably low price of $27,000 they could purchase a general purpose computer, limited in power, to be sure, but nonetheless a real computer. The price was achieved by a combination of several factors: a simple, classical, no-frills, logical design; a superior packaging technique for the electronic circuits; and, most important, use of a short word length. Most of the large computers of that era were using word lengths ranging from about 30 to 50 bits, the length being influenced by considerations of accuracy and instruction format. By cutting the word length to 12 bits, DEC was able to greatly reduce the hardware needed in the arithmetic unit. A short word length limits neither accuracy nor type of operations performed, but it often means that computation proceeds more slowly. For example, numerical computations may require cumbersome multiple precision routines in order to secure adequate accuracy. In simple terms, short word machines achieve low hardware costs at the expense of execution efficiency. Since there are many applications in which the slowest computer is still much faster than the application requires (e.g., a computer controlling a lathe) the loss of execution efficiency may not be important.

By 1966 DEC had sold 500 PDP 8s, and computer users were fiercely debating the issue of small dedicated computers versus timesharing systems. The controversy is by no means resolved, but there are many applications in which the two approaches are essentially noncompetitive. And, as Corey will make clear in the next paper, many of the configurations in use today combine features of the two approaches.

In 1969 the trade press began referring to small computers as "mini-computers"—terminology that may well have been influenced by the appearance of miniskirts on the fashion scene.

By 1970 DEC had sold 8,500 PDP 8s and the company's growth from three employees to over 6,000 provided a model for numerous competitors to emulate. Very often, a bright engineer with ambition would leave his computer-manufacturer employer, hire a few friends, borrow some capital and launch himself into the computer business. As evidence of this activity, thirty-six new brands and models of minicomputers were introduced in 1970. Most of these machines were perfectly respectable computers but with relatively little to differentiate brand X from brand Y.

The year 1971 was a rather cheerless one for the electronics industry as the abrupt reduction in government support of the space program brought widespread unemployment and business slowdowns. The one bright light on the economic horizon was the burgeoning minicomputer industry. The small size and low cost of the minis opened up a host of new applications ranging from the mundane (controlling traffic lights) to the exotic (voice recognition systems). In this phase of the development we see an interesting regenerative cause and effect relationship. New applications increase sales; increased sales permit production economics and lower prices; lower prices stimulate new applications. In mid-1974 we appear still to be in the regenerative development phase.

In 1972 Computer Automation, Inc. introduced a full-scale computer for less than $1,000. Of course, to achieve that price the NAKED MINI was marketed without cabinet and power supply (hence, the name), but that was entirely appropriate since these machines were intended for incorporation into larger pieces of electronic equipment. Once the $1,000 barrier was broken, it was easier to see the computer as a *component* (albeit a very sophisticated one) in a larger system. The NAKED MINI was also sold as a complete, free-standing computer (i.e., with cabinet and power supplies) for about $2,000.

Minicomputers are usually defined as being physically small, short word machines selling for less than a specified amount, i.e., $20,000. This seems to be a reasonable enough definition, but recent trends in hardware design—e.g., toward longer words—have confused the issue. The 12-bit word of the PDP 8 *is* restrictive in terms of instruction format and addressing, and thus, 16 bits has become a more popular word length. About 50 manufacturers make 16-bit machines, a handful make 18- and 24-bit machines. In 1973 Interdata announced a 32-bit computer with up to one million bytes of directly addressable core memory. This machine looks like a mini and with 32K bytes of core is priced like a mini at $9,950. On the other hand, it can be purchased with a million bytes of core for $171,650, a price well outside the range usually associated with minicomputers. Note also that the 32-bit word length is the same as that used in the IBM 360/370 series. This blurring of the distinction between minicomputers and large computers has resulted in the bizarre expression "mega-mini" to describe the larger minis.

The year 1973 was also one in which the POS (point of sale) market started having a substantial impact on the computer industry. Retailers began to see that by using computer terminals in place of cash registers they could gather more complete and timely data for better control. As an example, a typical grocery store computer terminal costs about the same as a mechanical cash register (about $2,500) but has a much more extensive and flexible set of functions, such as check verification. Typically, all the terminals in a store are connected to a minicomputer on the premises.

Many packaged food items now carry machine-readable uniform product codes in the form of a bar code printed on the package. Eventually most of the data entered at checkout stations will probably be from machine-readable labels rather than from hand keying. Libraries clearly should profit from this trend since input devices (such as light pens) developed for POS will be adaptable for library activities such as circulation. Although light pens are already in use in libraries, the widespread use of POS terminals should result in cheaper, more reliable equipment and some desirable standardization of data formats.

In the brief history given here I have tried to include examples illustrating significant trends in minicomputer development: minis are getting smaller, they are getting larger, they are becoming more versatile, and they are becoming more specialized. Thus the minicomputer manufacturers are attempting to fill every economic niche, much as Darwin's finches diversified to fill every ecological niche. One might call this adaptive radiation in the marketplace.

## WHAT'S NEW IN HARDWARE

### Addressing Schemes

One of the more conspicuous trends in computer hardware is that memories have gotten cheaper, larger and more complex in their organization.

For minicomputers, the increase in memory size has exacerbated a problem alluded to earlier—that a short instruction word just does not provide enough bits to specify a large number of addresses. Minicomputer designers have gotten around this problem with a variety of ingenious techniques. The address portion of the instruction may give an address directly, or relative to the present address, or within a "page" or specifying a new page, or where the real address can be found, etc. The last method is called indirect addressing and should be especially meaningful to librarians. When a librarian encounters a tracing card in the catalog with the rubber-stamped message "FOR LOCA-TION OF COPIES SEE AUTHOR OR MAIN ENTRY CARD," he or she is experiencing indirect addressing. That is, the tracing does not give the location of the book, it gives the location of the card bearing the location information.

A nonexhaustive search of manufacturers' literature reveals the Lockheed SUE as the champion in terms of addressing schemes. The SUE provides *seventeen* different addressing modes. This wealth of addressing schemes makes possible very clever and powerful programs, but it does nothing to simplify the work of the programmer. Corey will amplify this point in the following paper.

IBM's recent introduction of virtual storage in their machines might lead the casual observer to believe that VS had just been invented. Actually, VS goes back to a 1960 University of Manchester development and has been incorporated in large computers such as the Burroughs machines for several years. VS is just now beginning to make an appearance in minicomputers but there is every reason to feel that it will be a significant factor in the near future. Basically, VS is a system of automatically swapping information back and forth between disk and core so that the application program can access the entire disc memory space as if it were core. A simple example may help to clarify this. Imagine a small computer with 8 "pages" of core where a page is defined as 1,024 words. A program written for this machine might occupy 32 pages of memory with 8 pages in core and the other 24 on disk. During the execution of the program, memory access instructions covering the entire 32-page region are executed. If an address refers to one of the pages in core the program proceeds normally. If the program calls for an address from one of the disk pages, a "page fault" condition is raised. The VS system suspends execution of the program just long enough to transfer the needed page from disk to core. Since one of the core pages is overwritten by this operation, it is necessary to save that page by transferring it to disk before making the disk to core transfer. It is clear which page needs to be brought in from disk, but how does the VS system decide which core page is to be overwritten? The simplest and most common algorithm is to overwrite the *least recently used* page.

In principle, all this could be done on almost any machine by just writing a sufficiently clever operating system. Actually, VS is not feasible unless a good part of the work is done by hardware designed for the various VS functions. As an example, the *least recently used* function is more efficiently done with a hardware push-down stack than with a program.

The advantages associated with VS are substantial. For one thing, programmers can be freed from the grubby details of managing external files. Programmers generally would like their machine to have more core; VS does not give them more core, but it makes it possible for them to write their programs as if they had more core. A second advantage is that VS can minimize problems associated with machine expansion. Consider the previously cited machine having 8 pages of core and running a 32-page program. If an additional 8 pages of core is purchased it will be unnecessary to make any changes in the program. Independently of the amount of actual core, the program will run in 32 pages of virtual storage. The only effect on the program will be faster execution since fewer disc swaps will be needed.

## Input/Output

In early DEC literature the block diagram of the PDP 8 shows a single Teletype hanging on the accumulator. The Teletype was and is a modestly priced device suitable for limited I/O service. For PDP 8s used in classical scientific programming applications the Teletype was an adequate if not elegant solution to the problem of holding the cost down. Since that time minis have been used in a wide range of applications that require more sophisticated I/O facilities. The typical minicomputer sold today has an I/O bus that can accommodate up to 256 external devices. The bus can be thought of as a kind of party line (i.e., all the external devices are tied to the same set of wires) with a set of address lines to select a particular device and another set of lines for the data. Thus, when the CPU causes a message to be printed it merely specifies the printer on the address lines and the data on the data lines. But how does the input device get the attention of the CPU? The primitive way to handle this is to write a program that constantly interrogates the external device to see if it has anything to say. Thus, at some point in a circulation transaction the CPU would repeatedly ask the badge reader "Do you have another digit to give me?" Of course, the badge reader is pretty slow and the CPU is not getting much else done during this process.

The solution to this problem is provision of a hardware interrupt feature so that external devices can interrupt the program by causing a transfer of control to a special I/O routine. Following the interrupt, the interrupted program resumes. Very elaborate interrupt priority schemes are now available that permit device A to interrupt a background program, device B to interrupt device A, device C to interrupt device B, etc. An optional feature on some machines is an interrupt generated by a power failure. This interrupt is at the top of the priority list and transfers control to a special "tidying up" section of code that gets the machine ready for the return of power. Because of this, a lightning bolt in the neighborhood will not necessitate reloading the program. (The CPU has about 100 microseconds warning on a power failure, plenty of time to straighten out its affairs.)

Programmed data transfer, where the CPU controls I/O on a byte-by-byte basis, is fine for mechanical devices such as typewriters but is too slow for communication with high-speed devices such as magnetic tape, disc drives and other computers. With such high-speed devices the objective is usually to transfer fairly large blocks of information. To facilitate high-speed block transfers, many minicomputers now offer direct memory access as an optional extra. The DMA hardware is essentially a microcontroller interposed between the memory and the I/O bus. If a program requires that a block of data be transferred from core to disc (page swapping for example), the CPU transfers to the DMA the starting address in memory and the block size. Transfer of information can then proceed without executing an instruction for each word. Instead, each time the disc is able to accept a word, the DMA suspends execution of the main program for one memory cycle and uses that cycle to fetch the appropriate word. That way, transfer can proceed at a rate determined by the external device and at the same time interfere minimally with normal program execution. The trick of using a single memory cycle (which might come in the middle of an instruction) for this purpose is generally called "cycle stealing." Typical DMA transfer rates range up to about 1 million words/second.

## Instructions

One of the most effective ways for minicomputer manufacturers to compete is through the introduction of extensive and versatile instruction sets. As an example, the NAKED MINI can read punched paper tape with a two-instruction routine whereas the comparable NOVA requires a 24-instruction routine. Of course, it is not a question of how big the instruction set is, but rather how well it fits the application.

There are basically two ways of incorporating a set of instructions into a machine. The traditional method is to *wire* into the control unit the exact sequence of gating signals needed for each instruction. In other words, the instruction set is inextricably tied to the hardware design. In the *micro-programming* approach, a special read only memory *control store* is used to define the gating sequences. The execution of a particular instruction calls up a small section of the very high-speed ROM, and the control code for that instruction is simply a sequence of gating signals.

The most conspicuous advantage to microprogramming is that the instruction set of a particular machine can be tailored to the application. This may mean inclusion of fancy instructions (table search, error code generation and checking, etc.), and it can also mean adapting the instruction set to fit a particular compiler. At least one minicomputer is marketed in which a high-level language is available because it "fits" the instruction set.

At this writing the ultimate in microprogrammable machines is one in which a writable control store permits the end user of the computer to define the instruction set. Again, as Corey's paper will make clear, all this power and versatility does not necessarily make the computer easier to program.

## Peripherals

While it is true that the price of minicomputers has dropped sharply in recent years, the quoted low price of a computer may be misleading if "computer" refers to just the CPU. It is not uncommon for I/O and external storage devices to bring the total cost of a system up to triple the cost of the CPU. The high cost of peripherals has tended to limit applications of minicomputers, especially when peripherals designed primarily for large computers were used. The problem with standard, large-machine peripherals is that capacity, complexity and cost are all inappropriate for small, low-cost machines. Not too surprisingly, a wide range of peripherals developed expressly for minicomputers has appeared in recent months. Some of these devices are just simpler, slower versions of standard hardware—line printers capable of a few hundred lines/minute are a good example. Other peripherals developed for the minicomputer market do not have parallels in the big machine market and deserve brief mention.

As little as a few hundred dollars will now purchase a "floppy disk" system with a storage capacity in the few million bit range. The disk itself is a mylar disk housed in either an envelope or a small carton; cost of the disk is as little as $4.

Cassette tape transports use Phillips-type cassettes that superficially resemble the cassettes used in home tape recorders. Actually, the only real difference between audio cassettes and computer cassettes is that the latter are made to much higher quality standards. Cassette transports range from a few hundred to a few thousand dollars; storage on a cassette can range up to seven million bits. (In more graphic terms, a single shirtpocket-sized cassette might hold as much information as five boxes of tab cards.)

Several manufacturers offer tape cartridge systems that are rather diverse in terms of speed, capacity and cost. Comparisons between the various systems are made on the basis of these factors and many other details of construction such as physical size, adaptability to automatic changing, protection from dust, etc.

JAMES F. COREY
Systems Librarian
University of Illinois Library
Urbana-Champaign

# Configurations and Software: A Tutorial

This paper, together with the preceding paper by Divilbiss, is intended to provide a background for the characteristics of minicomputers and the ways in which they can be configured to tackle library problems. As part of the discussion of minicomputer features, an attempt is made to compare and contrast them with larger, general purpose computers. An acquaintance with basic computer concepts is assumed. Concepts of a more technical nature are explained as they are introduced. The first section below discusses configurations; the second section covers minicomputer software. Hardware and architectural features are covered in the paper by Divilbiss.

## MINICOMPUTER CONFIGURATIONS

Minicomputers and their associated peripheral devices can be combined in a great variety of ways, but this variety can be categorized into four basic configuration types: (1) stand-alone batch, (2) stand-alone on-line, (3) front end, and (4) remote concentrator.

The first type, stand-alone batch, is the most familiar (see figure 1). In this configuration, the mini looks like and performs like larger batch computers. In most cases the mini will have a card reader and punch, a line printer, tape drives and disks. (The minis in all four configuration types will have operator consoles, but to avoid cluttering the figures, the consoles have been omitted.) The term stand-alone is part of the name of this configuration in order to stress the fact that the mini is not connected to a larger computer. The mini stands alone. The main use of the stand-alone batch configuration is the generation of printed products, e.g., serials lists, purchase orders, circulation lists and overdue notices. This configuration could also be used for

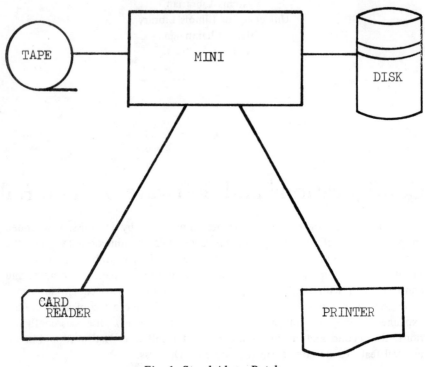

**Fig. 1. Stand-Alone Batch**

training librarians in programming techniques and machine operation and, in that capacity, might be of use to library schools as well as to libraries.

The second configuration, stand-alone on-line, is shown in figure 2. It has the peripheral devices used in the batch configuration but in addition has at least one kind of terminal device. Four common kinds of terminals are shown in the figure; cathode ray tubes and typewriters are two kinds shown attached to the mini. Both have keyboards and are used by library staff in "conversational mode" with the mini. Two kinds of circulation terminals are also shown. The one in the upper-left-hand corner of the figure represents the circulation terminal which reads Hollerith punched patron badges and book cards. The other terminal possesses the latest device, the "wand" reader, that can read coded strips about the size of a spine label. The strips may be magnetically coded or optically coded. The latter code is represented by a series of black and white stripes of varying thickness which can be interpreted by a light sensitive wand. An example of optically coded labels may be found

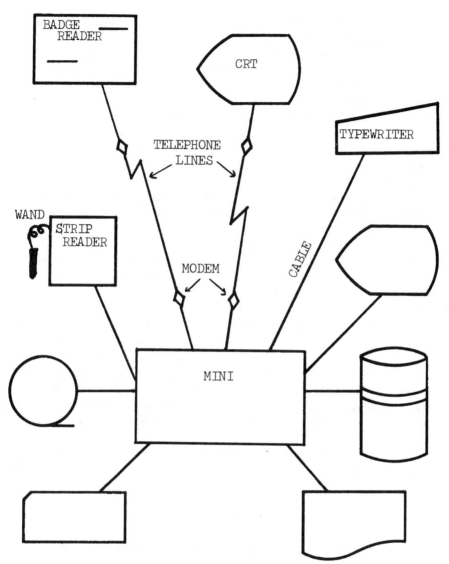

**Fig. 2. Stand-Alone On-Line**

on the side of an ordinary package of JELL-O. Whether optically or magnetically coded, the function of the labels is the same: they replace Hollerith
punched book cards and badges. Their main use to date has been in automated circulation systems.

Another kind of terminal not shown in figure 2 is the relatively slow (30-120 characters/second) remote printer. It can be paired with a CRT, or it can have its own line direct to the mini. In either case it would be used to produce on demand items such as purchase orders, vouchers, claim notices, book cards and spine labels.

Any of these terminals may be cabled directly to the computer or connected to it over telephone lines. Required speed of transmission, distance from terminal to mini, and costs are the three factors which determine the choice. A mixture of both types of connection may be present on the same machine, and this situation is shown in figure 2.

The stand-alone on-line mini can be used to assist with almost any library recordkeeping job. It can be used especially well in acquisitions, circulation, and serials check-in. However, in cataloging applications, two problems are encountered: character set and disk storage capacity. The character-set problem is not unique to the mini. It is really a terminal problem, and as such affects computer-assisted cataloging on any size machine. Currently, it is difficult to find terminal manufacturers who will provide character-sets that include diacriticals and special alphabetic characters found in foreign languages using the Roman alphabet.

The other problem, disk storage capacity, is unique to minicomputers. As the number of MARC records produced at the Library of Congress grows, so does the problem of storing them, plus the library's own original cataloging, on-line. Thus far, larger computers have kept up with the storage problem, while minis have not been able to do so. Storage capacity is expanding, however, as larger disks become available for minis. But for the moment, the ability of the mini to store large bibliographic files on-line is more promise than fact, and minicomputers installed in libraries are more successfully used for acquisitions, serials and circulation than for cataloging. Papers by Beaumont, Grosch, Brudvig and Lourey in this volume describe some actual uses of the mini in a stand-alone on-line configuration.

Both of the above stand-alone configuration types apply to large computers as well as to minis. But the point to be stressed here is that minis today are not harshly restrictive in the number and types of peripherals they can support. The only restriction lies in disk capacity and even that is disappearing. This is quite a contrast with the first minis which supported only an operator's console and a paper tape reader/punch!

The third configuration type is called the front end configuration and is shown in figure 3. The peripheral devices attached to the mini are the same as in the stand-alone on-line configuration. The difference is the addition, in the front end configuration, of another, usually larger, computer with which the

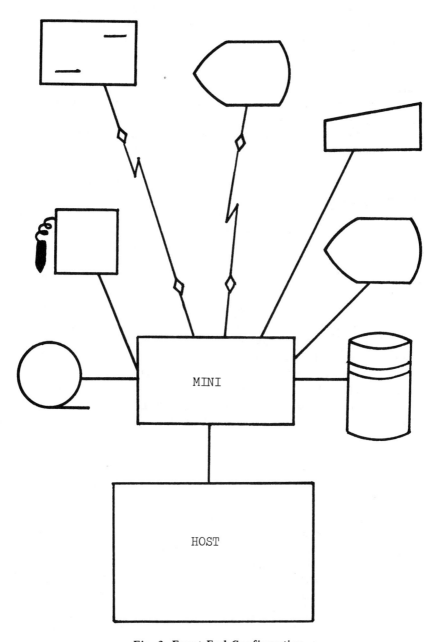

**Fig. 3. Front End Configuration**

mini communicates. The larger computer is usually called the host. The mini stands "in front" of the host, collects messages from the terminals, routes the messages to the host for processing and returns replies to the terminals. The mini is housed relatively close to the host and is usually connected to it by cable rather than by telephone line.

In its most basic use, the front end mini serves as a simpleminded communications link between terminals and host, i.e., the mini forwards what it receives. But invariably the mini is used to do more. It can be given the task of converting messages from disparate terminals into a common code and common format to make processing simpler for the host. It can handle errors in data transmission, asking for retransmissions and sending messages to the terminal operators when errors are identified as permanent equipment failures needing service repair. The mini can serve as back-up when the host is down by informing terminal operators and continuing to accept and store message requests for later processing when the host is again available.

Such tasks as the above are known as systems programs because they are designed to make the *computer system* as a whole perform as well as possible. Systems programs are not directly concerned with the particular work, expressed in the form of a particular message, that the terminal operator is trying to accomplish. Systems programs are contrasted with application programs. The latter are programs written to do a given job as seen from the point of view of the terminal user. For example, one terminal user may be preparing a purchase order; another may be discharging a book. For each of these transactions there would be an application program to fulfill the needs of that transaction. But a communications program written to get messages in and out without regard to the content of the message would be a system program.

There is no hard line between the two concepts. The communications program may have a small routine to check for valid transaction codes at the beginning of messages, rejecting invalid codes with an error message to the terminal rather than forwarding them to the host. The "system" program becomes just slightly application-oriented.

Front end minis are frequently programmed to execute a number of application programs in addition to basic systems programs. Small volatile files are often placed on the mini's disk, allowing the mini to handle some transactions completely. Brief circulation records containing only patron ID, call number, and due date, for instance, can be placed on the mini's disks, permitting charging and discharging to be done on the mini. Yet a request for an overdue notice would go to the host to access the bibliographic and patron data associated with the overdue. When front ends are programmed in this way, the configuration is also termed a distributed logic system because the logic of the application is distributed across more than one computer. Papers by Davison and Payne in this volume describe cases of minis used in a front end configuration.

A variation of the front end configuration is the network configuration shown in figure 4. Instead of communicating with terminals, the mini routes messages to other computers. The key function performed by a front end mini in a network is the translation of the machine language code of its host into a common communications code. By using a single communications code and front end minis, host computers from different manufacturers can be easily interconnected on the network. The much-heralded U.S. bibliographic network where each host serves as a state or regional node in the network has, so far, not materialized. When the network does materialize, it may be configured in the manner shown in figure 4. At present, the ARPA network in the United States[1] and the SITA airline reservations network in Europe,[2] two of the world's biggest, are configured in this manner.

The fourth and last configuration type is called the remote concentrator configuration (see figure 5). It is like the front end in practically every respect. The one essential difference is the location of the mini viz-à-viz the host. In the front end configuration, the mini is fairly close to the host and is connected to it by cable. In the remote concentrator configuration, the mini is farther away from the host and is connected to it by telephone line. The configuration gets its name because it is "remote" from the host and takes messages from several terminals and "concentrates" them over a single line to the host.

Other than the factor of distance, the same comments made above about front ends apply equally well to remote concentrators. Remote concentrators contain systems programs and, usually, application programs. They can provide back-up to the host, and they may process some transactions completely. The paper by Waite in this volume describes a minicomputer configured as a remote concentrator.

From this brief overview of minicomputer configurations, it should be apparent that there are many potential ways in which minis can be put to use to assist libraries with their data processing needs. But no mini will produce results for the library until it is properly programmed.

## MINICOMPUTER SOFTWARE

In the area of minicomputer software, it is hazardous to state generalizations because the situation is changing so rapidly. Manufacturers of

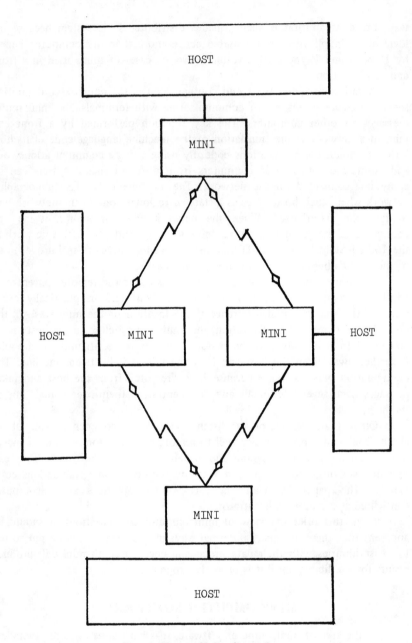

**Fig. 4. Network Configuration**

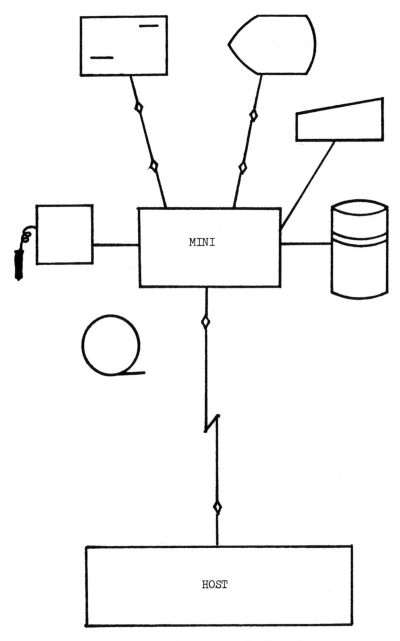

**Fig. 5. Remote Concentrator Configuration**

minicomputer hardware, as well as independent software firms, are steadily bringing out new programs or enhancements to old programs. Nonetheless, it might be worthwhile to summarize the present and identify trends for the future. As with configurations, an effort will be made to indicate similarities and differences between minicomputer software and large computer software.

In the computer business there is a commonly used saying: "Hardware is potentiality; software is actuality." The expression means that the hardware provides the potential to solve a problem, but well-written, thoroughly tested software is required to make the solution actual. This is understandable in light of the way computers are marketed. The hardware manufacturer builds the computer and provides some basic systems software consisting of two main components—an operating system and some number of programming languages. The customer, using the support of the operating system and the programming languages, writes programs (application programs) to solve his own set of problems. As purchased, the machine has only the potential to do useful work for the buyer. This situation is equally true for minicomputers and large computers.

The question arises: "How hard is it to achieve actuality?" The answer, expressed in terms of cost, is: "Very hard." Over the past ten years the cost of hardware has been steadily dropping while programming costs have been steadily increasing. The computer facility manager finds a greater percentage of his budget going to personnel each year. With respect to minicomputer users, a study has shown that the ratio of software costs to hardware costs is running two to one.[3] Software costs are twice the hardware costs! "Actuality" does not come cheaply.

The objective of the cost-conscious minicomputer user, then, should be to strive to get as much software support from the hardware manufacturer or other commercial source as possible. First, take the minicomputer hardware manufacturer. What software does he furnish? It can be categorically stated that no minicomputer manufacturer provides what could even remotely be called an automated system for libraries. There is no package from any manufacturer that will order library materials, receive them, pay for them, catalog them or circulate them. Library application programs must be written by the customer. Admittedly, some library packages are available from independent firms, but these firms were first of all customers of the hardware manufacturer, and, as such, had to take the software provided by the manufacturer and develop the application using what was useful of the manufacturer's systems software. Let us consider then the manufacturers' software to see what will help the developer of library applications. In explaining manufacturers' software, the progression will be from the simplest versions to the most complex. This approach is not only easier, it also recapitulates the history of minicomputer software. The software was initially very basic, but it has been improving steadily. The information on manufacturers' software was derived from brochures and technical manuals supplied by several minicomputer manufacturers and from a survey of a number of books and articles on minicomputers, the most notable of which is one by Auerbach.[4]

The first minis had quite rudimentary input and output devices—one operator console and one paper tape reader/punch. This configuration is still available and is called the paper tape mini. The software is commensurate with the rudimentary hardware. It consists of four programs. The first program is a bootstrap loader which has to be laboriously dialed into memory by setting switches and pushing buttons on the front panel of the mini. The bootstrap loader does one thing: it loads the second program—the real loader. The loader in turn loads the third program—the assembler. The assembler and loader are on paper tape, so merely getting the programs into memory is time consuming. At ten characters/second, the standard speed of some paper tape readers, a 4,000 character assembler takes over six minutes just to load. The assembler reads and translates an application program and punches it on paper tape. The loader then loads the application program and, if the latter fails, the fourth vendor-supplied program—the debugger—is loaded. The debugger can write to the operator console, printing values from the collapsed program to assist the programmer in diagnosing the problem.

The assembler furnished in the vendor package is itself quite basic. It cannot accept macros or external names and it does not produce relocatable code. Space does not allow an accurate explanation of macros, external names and relocatable code, but a rough explanation is possible.

A macro is a single written instruction that translates into several machine instructions. Without macros the programmer has to write down one instruction for every instruction the machine is to execute. With macros, any group of instructions that is frequently executed together can be symbolized by a shorthand notation—a macro. Whenever the programmer wants that group of instructions, he can write the macro and the assembler will expand it into its corresponding group of instructions.

External names are names not defined in the program. They allow programs to be broken into separately written modules which have the ability to communicate with each other. One module can refer by name to an item of data in another module as long as the assembler knows the data item is external. Without support for external names, program modules could not talk to one another, thus defeating most of the purpose of modular programming.

Relocatable code is code that can be placed anywhere in the machine and still run. It is contrasted with absolute code which will run at only one place in computer memory. This one place must be known in advance to the assembler. A control card is furnished to the assembler, stating, for example, that the program is to begin at main memory location 2370. Absolute code, besides forcing programs to fit in certain places, makes modular programming difficult. It is seldom possible to know in advance how big modules will be. If modules A, B, and C are eventually to come together to make one program, module B must fit after module A. Since the final size of A cannot be known in advance, the starting location of module B cannot be specified.

Modular programming permits division of labor because several programmers can work on separate modules of a total program. Modular programming also permits frequently used subroutines to be saved and combined into new programs. External names and relocatable code, by supporting modular programming, and macros, by supporting code efficiency, all help to increase programmer productivity. The basic assembler, lacking these features, causes longer development time and higher development costs.

A mini with only a console and paper tape for input/output is of no value to libraries because the input and output is too limited. A minimal increase producing a useful machine is the addition of communications lines and terminals. The mini can then be attached to a host to become a front end or remote concentrator. However, unless the software is improved, program preparation will still be difficult, hence, costly.

The next step up in vendor-supplied software is the improvement of program preparation software, a phrase that refers to the subset of programs supplied by the vendor which are used most often in the preparation of new programs. Besides the assembler, program preparation software includes other language translators, a program called a linkage editor and a set of programs known as utilities. The first improvements are usually made to the assembler. The vendor makes the assembler capable of accepting macros, external names and generating relocatable code. Relocatable code, as mentioned, allows programs to be written in modules; but the existence of modules introduces a new problem. To function as a total program the modules must be "linked" together by the linkage editor, the program which unites modules. It is run after the assembler is finished. It uses external names to link referenced items with referencing instructions, and it relocates relocatable code to make all modules contiguous.

Another assist for the programmer is a set of utilities. Utilities are off-line programs best explained by examples of their functions:

1. moving data from cards to tape or vice versa,
2. moving data from cards to disk or vice versa,
3. moving data from tape to disk or vice versa,
4. moving data from cards, tape or disk to the printer,
5. combining two files of data into one,
6. splitting one file into two,
7. inserting new data into the middle of an existing file, or
8. deleting selected data from a file.

If the data are programs or a string of program instructions, the utilities can be seen as instruments to create and modify programs. Utilities are also used to maintain a program library. A program library is a set of individual files (programs) with an index which tells the location and size of each program or program module. Program libraries are accessed by the linkage editor to retrieve modules for linking into programs. Program libraries are also used to store the macros accessed by the assembler to convert the single macro instruction into a set of real instructions.

The next improvement in program preparation software is usually a higher-level language. The most commonly offered is FORTRAN, followed by BASIC, both numerically oriented languages. COBOL is beginning to be available on a few machines, while PL/1 is nonexistent on minis. All higher level languages support external names and relocatable code. By their very nature, they do not need macros.

If the minicomputer is very small and its I/O capacity limited, e.g., a front end mini with no tape or disk, the program preparation programs are very slow and cumbersome to run on the mini. The higher level language translators may even require more main memory than the mini has available. To alleviate this problem, vendors often supply language translators, linkage editors and utilities that run on large, general purpose machines, but which, nevertheless, produce programs that run on the mini. This concept is often difficult to understand. The programs are written in the mini's language. They are translated on a different machine, but the output of the translation process is machine code for the mini that will run only on the mini. The machine code will not run on the translating machine. It has to be physically transported to the mini for execution. The machine code could be punched into cards, and read into the mini through its card reader. Another technique is used at the University of Illinois where an IBM System/7 is connected by cable to an IBM 370/158. The System/7's programs are assembled and link edited on the 158 and then sent by a utility over the cable to the System/7. Program preparation on a different machine is called cross-assembly.[5]

Cross-assembly is not limited to machines from the same vendor. Since most mini vendors do not make large computers, their cross-assemblers necessarily run on computers of other vendors.

The next hardware expansion applied to a mini is the addition of tapes, disk, card readers and line printer. These I/O devices greatly increase the mini's power. The program preparation software no longer needs to be run on another machine. The language translators, program libraries, linkage editor and utilities can be run on the mini. Additional software can also be provided.

At this stage, an input/output control system appears. The two most important sets of routines in the IOCS are the peripheral drivers and the interrupt handlers. Both sets of routines do I/O at the physical level, i.e., they are concerned with status bits that are set on and off by the hardware as electrical signals are sent back and forth between the CPU and its peripherals. Bits can be set to indicate a variety of conditions: device ready, device busy, temporary error, permanent error, request completed, etc. Peripheral drivers are responsible for initiating I/O operations. When the operation successfully starts, they are finished. There is one routine for each type of device because the meaning of the bit settings can vary from device to device. The routines are "device dependent." The interrupt handlers are responsible for processing an I/O operation when it is complete. The term interrupt handlers is used because most computers are designed so that an electrical signal is sent to the CPU by the peripheral on completion of the I/O event. The signal interrupts the CPU to call attention to the completed event. Like peripheral drivers, interrupt handlers are device dependent.

The value of an IOCS is in its assistance to programmers. Programmers can then do I/O on the logical level instead of the physical level. Instead of testing bits, the programmer writes a statement which says, in effect: "Here is a record. Write it to tape drive number three, and tell me when you are done."

With IOCS, programmers need never know which bit settings mean what—except in one circumstance. Vendors are very good about providing peripheral drivers and interrupt handlers for their own peripherals as it makes the peripherals easy to use. However, they usually make it a policy not to provide such routines for peripherals of competitive vendors. When a user wants to connect company X's terminal to company Y's mini, extra programming for the peripheral driver and interrupt handler must be done, adding to costs and development time.

Another systems software feature is known as a console command language. It is a set of commands that the operator can type in on the console to cause programs already in the main memory of the mini, or in a predesignated program library, to be executed. This saves the programmer from having to put batches of cards in a card reader every time he wants to run a standard program. Translators and utilities are some of the programs callable from the console via the command language. Another program callable may be a text editor, a program which will retrieve lines of text from a file, allow the operator to correct the text by inserting or deleting characters or whole lines, and return the corrected lines to the file. A text editor is, in effect, an on-line version of one of the utilities. Since programs can be treated as lines of text, the existence of a text editor increases programmer productivity by allowing for faster program correction.

A better debugging program is usually furnished for minis that have line printers. Extensive information about the state of the machine at the time of failure can be printed very quickly. This feature is very important both for new programs in the testing stage and for operational ones which encounter an unforeseen combination of circumstances causing a malfunction.

The software features that have been described to this point are summarized in table 1. Two minis that have most of these features are the IBM System/7 and the Datapoint. Minis with these capabilities can do a great deal of valuable work. They can perform in any of the four configurations described earlier. Their main limitation is that they cannot run more than one program simultaneously, i.e., they do not permit multiprogramming. For example, a mini with the software described thus far could not run a circulation system on-line and concurrently test a new book fund accounting program. The circulation program would have to be stopped first and removed from the machine. Testing becomes inconvenient for the programmer who wants to develop a second application. Testing would begin when the library closed.

To alleviate this limitation, many mini vendors offer some form of multiprogramming operating system. Most frequently offered is the ability to run two programs simultaneously. A few vendors support three simultaneous programs, but few go beyond three. In contrast, large machine operating systems may support fifty. When the mini vendor supports two programs, the terminology used is foreground-background. The foreground is given first priority by the operating system. The background takes over only when the foreground is waiting. Returning to the above example, the operational on-line circulation system could run in the foreground while the book fund accounting program under development could be run in the background.

Allowing multiprogramming requires a much more sophisticated operating system. The basic problem is this: both programs want the same resources —the CPU, all of main memory and all of the peripherals. The operating

Paper Tape Software
  Bootstrap loader
  Loader
  Assembler (no macros, no external names, absolute code)
  Debugger

Program Preparation Software (runs on host or mini with disk)
  Assembler (macros, external names, relocatable code)
  Linkage editor
  Program library
  FORTRAN
  BASIC
  COBOL

Disk-Oriented Software
  Input/Output Control System (IOCS)
  Console command language
  Text editor
  Better debugger

**Table 1. Vendor Supplied Software**

system has to arbitrate the application programs' demands for these resources. The solution in the case of the CPU has already been described. The program entered into the machine as the foreground program gets priority on the CPU. Only when the foreground releases the CPU does the background get it.

Main memory management must fulfill two functions: it must allocate storage and it must protect allocated storage from aggrandizement by over-zealous programs. Storage allocation algorithms vary from machine to machine. Some are quite dynamic, expanding and contracting program space as the program runs. Others are static, giving the program one fixed piece of memory for the duration of the run. Reasons for the diffferent approaches are beyond the scope of this paper, but one of the most sophisticated, called virtual memory, is explained by Divilbiss in the preceding paper. Storage protection is a combination of hardware and software which defends allocated storage by canceling the offending program and booting it from the machine. The reason for cancellation is printed in a diagnostic report; cancellation is usually because of errors in programming that cause a program to try to store data outside its allotted area. Storage protection routines must keep any application program from reaching beyond its bounds in order to prevent damage to other application programs or even to the operating system.

Probably the most complex arbitration work required of the multi-programming system is the allocation of devices. Most programs want to read cards, print messages and write on tapes and disks. Running the purchase order program and the overdue notices program simultaneously without device allocation is likely to result in the patron's overdue notice going to a bookdealer and the book order going to the patron. Methods for dealing with device allocation vary, but usually each program is required to state prior to execution what devices it needs. If all devices are available, they are assigned to the program and it proceeds. If not all devices are available, the program is either held up or it proceeds using temporary substitute devices, with the data being moved to the correct device later by the operating system.

Many mini vendors offer operating systems with multiprogramming. Digital Equipment Corporation, Hewlett Packard, Varian, and Data General, to name a few, have advanced their software to this stage. And these operating systems are continually being improved. Mini operating systems, formerly primitive, are now approaching the level of complexity of operating systems available on medium-sized, general-purpose computers.

In summary, minis have made dramatic improvements in the past ten years, both in price reduction and in hardware and software capabilities. For library work minis are still weak in several areas. They are weak in the higher level languages best suited to variable length strings of alphabetic characters. PL/1 is not supported. Character-string features in COBOL are not supported. Minis are still somewhat limited in their support of large capacity disks, and they are weak in the support of indexes to large data files. But if the previous ten years is any guide, limitations will disappear. Front end and remote concentrator minis are already working in several libraries. Stand-alone minis are also doing specialized library jobs such as book fund accounting and circulation. In the future, stand-alone minis may be dedicated to libraries, assisting them in all facets of library bibliographic control.

## REFERENCES

1. Sher, Michael S. "A Case Study in Networking," *Datamation*, 20:56-59, March 1974.

2. Hirsch, Phil. "SITA: Rating a Packet-Switched Network," *Datamation*, 20:60-63, March 1974.

3. Ross, D. T. "Software Development for Minicomputers." In *Minicomputers: International Computer State of the Art Report* (Infotech State of the Art Report, no. 13). Maidenhead, Berkshire, England, Infotech Information Ltd., 1973, pp. 203-26.

4. Auerbach, Inc. *Auerbach on Minicomputers*. New York, Petrocelli, 1974.

5. Lamb, Vincent S. "All About Cross-Assemblers," *Datamation*, 19:77-80, July 1973.

WALTER W. CURLEY
President, Gaylord Brothers
Syracuse, New York

# The Minicomputer and the Computer Gap for Libraries

Much has been written on the use of computers in libraries but until recently the promise has exceeded the performance. Colleges and universities, by virtue of equipment on campus and the fact that in many instances research-oriented faculties were present, made progress through the 1960s and even into the early 1970s. Public libraries found it considerably more difficult and their progress was mostly with tab card equipment in which they struggled with report-oriented systems. For decades transaction card circulation control systems using the punched card in one form or another have been used in a variety of libraries, both public and academic.

Many libraries found it difficult to move upward from tab equipment because of the problem of size and cost of the computer, and the lack of sophistication of staff necessary in-house to cope with the new demands made by the next level of computer. In the last five years—perhaps really the last three—minicomputers and time-sharing, which can compliment the efforts of the minicomputer or act as a competitor, have provided libraries with the ability to not only move up to the next level of sophistication, but to do so without dramatically increasing the costs to the library.

Networking appears to be on the verge of becoming a reality. Certainly OCLC, BIBNET, the program developed at Stanford University, NELINET, the Medical Library Program and others all point to the fact that networks are either here or just around the corner. Either networks or minis can fill a need to receive answers, not just reports, and to develop fast turn-around response time to questions that, when the answers were provided from a card file, were provided within a matter of minutes.

The mini can either act as a terminal or stand alone as a computer. Dozens of manufacturers in the United States are providing the hardware which is dramatically reducing in size and at the same time reducing costs. Minis are becoming the fastest sellers in the computer business. On the consumer side, for example, is a new jogging computer. At prototype licensing stage this simple, tiny computer strapped to belt or wrist keeps a jogger informed of his progress via buzzer and floating crystal dial.

IBM predicts that 50 percent of the manufacturer outlays for automation equipment by the mid-1970s will be for minicomputers. *Business Week* says that the $2000 minicomputer of today equals the $100,000 machine of a decade ago.

My first exposure to a minicomputer occurred five years ago when I was in the employ of a large consulting firm. It was important for that firm to be able to charge correctly costs related to any client's account. For example, a telephone call made on behalf of a client should be charged to that client's account. At that time, independent of the telephone company, a minicomputer was available which would capture the dialed information, telephone number charges, client number, etc., store it, and daily feed it into a large computer which was on the premises. It provided the ability to capture the information and, by also providing the storage facility, allowed the material to be transferred at a minimum of cost and interruption of service.

A firm in the mailing machine business has produced and is selling a machine which will weigh a package, automatically produce the right amount of stamps via a postage meter and provide backup information, such as item shipped, date, cost, destination, etc., which then can be transported back to the basic computer. The machine consists of the usual conveyor belts, etc. but contains within it a small minicomputer which does the work and is supposed to be accident- and mistake-free. The operator merely indicates the area code and selects a United Parcel, U.S. mail, or foreign shipment button and the program takes over. The processing and estimates as to the amount of stamps, etc. normally would have been done by people and would have been subject to a certain percentage of error. The producer claims that the machine is not only 50 percent faster but will pay for itself in one year due to the number of errors, etc. that will be eliminated. The machine also provides a unique number, which is put on each package, which will allow for controls to be developed when it becomes necessary to trace a package which is lost, damaged, strayed or stolen. This machine is really not very far away from a circulation control device which libraries could use, and with minor adaptations might find a role in the library field. There are now many examples of minicomputers being used in the library field principally in the areas of acquisitions, circulation control and/or budget and personnel functions.

A major competitor for the mini is time-sharing, which may or may not be used in conjunction with a minicomputer using as terminals either cathode ray tube or other, with direct or indirect lines into a computer located elsewhere and paying for the storage cost. At Gaylord Brothers this is the present approach for the internal management work load.

It seems that as the mini becomes smaller and less costly and density of storage increases, the competitor for the mini is going to be the terminal. In other words, it seems that the computer, as being used by libraries, will either become much smaller or libraries will avail themselves of the very large computers which are particularly useful in storing massive amounts of information (data banks) and, of course, where networks are being used. Whether to use a mini or a terminal has to do with cost and that depends to a certain degree on the type of use.

There are implications here for the way in which total systems are being contemplated and will be contemplated in the future. There are very few total systems, and most prudent administrators find it necessary to have thresholds of achievement visible at regularly stated intervals. This is important because of the money involved and the frequently low tolerance level on the part of boards and trustees when one begins to talk in terms of six-, eight- or ten-year pay-outs. Developing systems piece-meal or on a modular basis using mini-computers and/or the time-sharing approach can be considerably easier and still allow for a system approach to become operational on a full-blown basis. This would make computers available to libraries to cope with problems that have needed resolution for many years. It should allow for systems to be re-developed at the end of five, six, seven years—whenever they become obsolete—at a minimal cost. The former solution usually was to upgrade to more expensive equipment. The new approach should allow the library to take advantage of vastly improving technology which in five, six or seven years ought to reduce the cost considerably and make the solutions now achieved even more desirable and palatable.

Library functions other than the major ones—circulation, acquisitions, etc.—are important and yet serve almost discreet functions. For example, the audiovisual department or film bureau may need a reservation system to schedule use of materials well in advance, always maintaining knowledge of their present location. There is a limited number of items (perhaps several thousand) to be found in the audiovisual collections of many libraries. The need for information and fast turn-around in these libraries is provided by clerks rather expensively and often inadequately.

Service to the blind entails a discreet number of borrowers, a well-defined collection, a need for an accurate reservation system and quick response. There are at least fifty such institutions offering this service. Cleveland Public Library, for example, mails out 1000 talking books per day and, with less than 10,000 talking books in supply, there is need for eliminating delays and for the ability to respond quickly when telephone calls requesting reservations are received. The reader usually makes known his need via telephone or mail, and mailing of items is the usual delivery system. A reader profile, including reader interest, is often maintained. Use of a minicomputer with software providing a matrix allowing for a reservation system is not only a possibility but a reality.

One problem, particularly in libraries, is that batch-oriented systems with centralized processing units do not readily succumb to decentralization. People are involved and a level of sophistication is involved. This is a problem that should not be minimized. Placing a minicomputer in an order department and with it the responsibility for producing on it means that the computer is visible and accountability is squarely placed within the department. It places the responsibility on the head of that department to manage it and it eliminates the remote fall guy (the centralized unit).

I have had personal experience with one minicomputer system in a traditional area of library service—acquisitions. As an administrator I felt the need of a mechanized system that provided information when needed and for specific questions. Report-oriented systems provide reams of paper which, when produced, frequently indicate the state of things three weeks ago and then become increasingly less useful with the passing of each day. It is important to an administrator to obtain quick response to questions like: What books have been held in cataloging over thirty days? or What is the status of a branch book budget this week?; or to have an *automatic* assignment of vendors, cancellation of dated orders or breakouts on any one of dozens of data compilations to answer specific questions. The minicomputer offers opportunity to the sophisticated and nonsophisticated in computerese to cope with the needs of the day both inexpensively and efficiently.

The library world has accepted change slowly. The minicomputer is at hand and with it, at last, comes the opportunity to provide mechanization to many library activities in segments but on a scale previously not practical. It deserves careful consideration, and opens the door for a major thrust forward and continued progress for and by librarians.

WALTER G. HAMNER

Assistant Director of Libraries
for Automation Services
University of Maryland
McKeldin Library
College Park, Maryland

# The Minicomputer and its Use in Library Operations at the University of Maryland

Minicomputers are being put to work in many different environments. With every repetitive paper handling task, there is a potential minicomputer application.

According to a recent study by International Data Corporation, publishers of *EDP Industry Report*, worldwide shipments of minicomputers will jump almost 50 percent this year, to a shipped value of $835 million.[1] By 1977, minis should represent a $2.5 billion business. Some promising fields are: business and banking, where mini-based point-of-sale and accounting systems are just beginning to tap the potential of autotransaction; support of data entry systems and telecommunications networks, where minis are used for message-switching; automated manufacturing, where minis are used in closed-loop systems; and customized packages that give sophisticated users clusters of inexpensive minis for on-line jobs that once required large machines. Minis are being shipped at a rate of 2,800 per month, and the installed population will outnumber general-purpose computers before the end of 1974. IDC expects that within five years the mini shipment rate will be 10,000 per month. The marketplace for minis is diffused, fragmented, and hard to define. Most manufacturers sell their machines as *tools*—most minis are dedicated to a single function. Currently, 58 percent of minis—and 96 percent of mini-peripherals—produced in the United States go to OEM suppliers. Potential end-users of minis are attracted by their increasing ease of use, even more than by their declining prices. Larger memories allow programming in higher level languages, rather than in machine languages. For example, Microdata has just announced a new small business system programmable in simple English sentences. Raytheon has announced a new mini that will be available on a rental basis, and a new mini array processor ($57,000) that can add two arrays of more than 16,000 numbers each into a third array, from a single instruction, and twenty times faster than the CPU could do the job under standard program control. The mini market currently supports at least fifty viable suppliers. IBM has not really entered the mini market, but rumors persist of a "System/2." If it ever appears, a true IBM minicomputer could change the shape of the industry.

An important educational application involves the effective use of minicomputers to handle the acquisition and circulation systems in university libraries.

The study of minicomputers and their successful application to library data processing should certainly include a review of the Singer Company's System 10 minicomputer[2] and point of transaction terminal system in use at McKeldin Library at the University of Maryland.

We feel that we have taken an innovative approach to the library's biggest headache—effective circulation control—without impairing service to our students, faculty or staff.

Before detailing how the system operates, let me first give some background on the University of Maryland and the kind of decentralized library system that it operates.

The University of Maryland is the seventh largest university system in the United States. The College Park, Maryland campus, where McKeldin Library is located, is the third largest campus in the United States. In 1972-73 it served an enrollment of 35,000 students with over 7,000 faculty and staff members, and the university is continuing to grow.

McKeldin Library is the central library of the university. It contains reference works, periodicals, circulating books, and other materials in all fields of research and instruction. The university library system, with its five branches, has nearly 2 million volumes and 19,000 active subscriptions to serials, periodicals and newspapers, plus a large collection of government documents, phonorecords, films, and filmstrips. The branch libraries include: the undergraduate library which houses 200,000 volumes; the engineering and physical sciences library which includes 200,000 volumes for engineering, physics, chemistry, biology, and botany studies; the architecture library with 50,000 volumes; and the College of Library and Information Services library with 40,000 volumes.

The central McKeldin Library with 900,000 volumes for faculty and graduate students, plus the university's main reference section, is also open to undergraduates. About 100,000 books may be out on loan at any one time, reflecting an in/out transaction rate that can approach 10,000 a day.

The demand for library services has nearly quadrupled in the last ten years. The student enrollment, which is increasing at a rate of 5 percent per year, has nearly doubled in the last ten years. In 1963 the enrollment was less than 20,000 and the library contained 550,000 volumes. During the following ten-year period the book budget also increased from $400,000 to over $2 million per year.

The Singer System 10 is not our first attempt to automate the library's circulation; in fact, the library has utilized a computer in its circulation operation for more than eight years. However, we do think that this Singer approach is our most effective to date in providing better service to our patrons and improved control for the librarians.

Immediate benefits of our new system include faster charging, discharging, recalling, and sending out overdue notices more promptly than in the past, operating our personal reserve system more efficiently, and garnering statistics on use that enable faster purchase of additional copies that are in demand.

When we are able to go to an on-line system that will provide round-the-clock input and access to data, rather than our present batching operation, we will be able to provide even faster service.

An important requirement for this kind of program is the up-to-date information from the university administration for the user address file. If this information is kept current, the library can notify a borrower that the book he charged out the day before is needed for a class reserve. But current address data are vital to assuring that borrowers will receive immediate notification. Our file of 55,000 names and addresses is entirely updated four weeks after the start of each semester and changes are received continually.

McKeldin Library's first attempt to automate its circulation system was in 1965 when an IBM 357 data collection system was installed. The system desired by the staff was one that would be simple enough for effective operation by clerical staff members and student assistants, yet sophisticated enough to provide a fully mechanized circulation control record that would include charging, discharging, personal reserve requests and recalls, overdue book notices, fines, statistics, and certain essential internal reports. It was apparent from the beginning that equipment installation would not constitute a major problem because the university's College Park campus had a centralized library.

The equipment configuration that was felt best suited to afford the library an effective circulation control system consisted of three IBM 357 input stations, each with a card and badge reading unit; three Model 372 manual entry units on-line with the card and badge reader input stations; one Model 358 input control; one 373 punch switch; and two modified 026 print card punches on-line with the 357 system.

The source documents used in the circulation system were prepunched identification badges and book cards. A student obtained his identification badge the first time he registered. It was validated automatically thereafter at the beginning of each semester until he left the university. A faculty or staff member, or any other person entitled to a badge, received one on request. When a book was processed, a book card was prepunched and placed in a pocket at the back of each book.

Considering the limitations of unit record equipment, this system was relatively effective. Certainly it was an improvement over the previous manual system. But it soon became apparent that it could not keep pace with the growth of the university and the related demands on the library. The 357 was replaced in 1967 by a more powerful IBM 1030 system.

In September 1968 we switched to a computer tape system with the installation of a UNIVAC 9300 computer. The flexibility and speed of the new computer enabled us to add another service to our patrons. Each day, the entire circulation master file is printed out on a high-speed printer. This printout indicates the call number of all books along with the social security number of the borrower. By reference to this printout a borrower can determine whether any given book should be on the shelf or is out on loan. This eliminates much time-consuming searching of the stacks to determine the availability of a given book.

Another feature of the system improved our personal reserve procedure. If the circulation printout indicates that a volume is out on loan, a potential borrower can fill out a personal reserve card on which he requests that he be notified when a specific book is returned. Data identifying the patron and the book to be held are recorded in the system on a daily basis and reserved books are automatically identified and segregated prior to their return to the shelves. The requestor is automatically notified of the availability of the reserved book and of the fact that the book will be held seven days for him.

The computer not only modernized the library's circulation operation, but it also produced timely and meaningful statistics including analysis of year-to-date circulation by type of patron (undergraduate, graduate, staff, faculty, etc.), type of book borrowed, as well as costs of books purchased by type.[3]

The UNIVAC 9300 configuration included a processor with 32,000 bytes of core memory, a 600 line/minute printer, a card reader and six magnetic tape drives with communication devices which enabled the library to interface its systems with the University of Maryland's UNIVAC 1108 located in the Computer Sciences Center.

Improvement in our backroom operations led us to take a closer look at improving the front end. One of the limitations of our 1030 terminals was the inability to edit input data at the source. This resulted in a great many inaccuracies getting into the system.

A key factor in our switch to the Singer System 10 data collection system was the ability of the Model 100 job information station terminals to purify input data. By using optical readers rather than sensor readers, the Singer terminals can edit data before it reaches the processor.

Up to ten transaction programs may be permanently resident within each Model 100 terminal and the programs may differ from one terminal to another. In addition each Model 100 can call up any of ninety programs from a disk-resident library. Another important factor is speed. The cycle time of the Singer terminals is four times greater than our previous system.

In the fall of 1972 we installed ten Model 100 terminals: four in the main McKeldin Library (two for charging and two for discharging), four in the undergraduate library, one in physical sciences, and one in library sciences. We expect to soon add another terminal in the architecture library.

The terminals feed data directly to a Singer System 10 processor with 30K of core memory, a Model 40 disk drive with 10 million characters of storage, and a Model 45 tape drive. Incoming transaction data are stored on the disk which, in addition to the current day's transaction file, also houses the preceding day's transactions, a master file of 55,000 user social security numbers, a books-on-reserve file, and system software. To protect incoming data, the System 10 records information simultaneously on disk and tape, so if one goes down, the other one is available to reconstruct data.

Input to the current system continues to come from badges and book cards. The Hollerith coded badges are embossed with the patron's name and nine-digit social security number, followed by a tenth digit which indicates whether the borrower is an undergraduate, graduate, faculty or staff. Each category of patron can take out books for different periods of time. The 80-column card residing in each book bears the LC classification number and circulation number.

In addition to accepting badges and cards through separate slots for optical reading, the Singer terminals will accept input data, instructions and queries through a numerical keyboard and function keys. Operators are guided in entering information by messages flashed on the terminal's display screen indicating the next step to be taken.

The terminal mask lists the various types of transactions the system will handle. The variables in each type of transaction are clearly spelled out, so that the terminal operator is led through each transaction in the proper sequence.

The Singer input stations are programmed to perform the following transactions: charge, renewal, emergency charge, discharge, place personal reserve, claims returned, patron inquiry and special transactions which include paid discharge, emergency discharge, lost book, patron inquiry on keyboard, personal reserve cancel, place search, search reply, payment reply, delayed discharge, message flag, message clear and enter dates. The special transactions can only be accomplished by a designated supervisor with an authority badge.

In a charge transaction, the social security number on the badge is checked against the master file on the disc, while book card data are checked for validity against the circulation file. In addition, the input station number is checked against the location number on the book card. Cleared data go to the transaction file. Otherwise, the Model 100 indicates failed data checks.

To understand how this works, let us follow the sequence of a typical charge-out. The terminal operator indicates a charge transaction by depressing button "0" and the charge light comes on. He then enters the patron's badge. The computer edits the badge to assure validity. If the borrower is not on file, this message is returned as a one-digit code in the terminal display, and the borrower is automatically added to the file. If the borrower's address file is incorrect or incomplete, the terminal operator is instructed to obtain this information before proceeding.

When the computer accepts the badge as a valid entry, the "insert book card" light comes on and again the terminal performs a four-step edit to check the call number field and the circulation number field. It also checks to assure that the book is not on reserve. When accepted, the "insert book card" lights again to see if more than one book is being checked out. If not, a cancel key ends the transaction and completes the charge-out procedure.

The renewal transaction is similar with the terminal again checking that the book has not been reserved by another patron and is not overdue, which would require payment of a fine.

To discharge books, the terminal operator inserts the book card and the computer checks for valid circulation number, correct location (that the book is being returned to the correct library) and if it is on reserve or overdue, which triggers the fine notice procedure.

To enter a personal reserve, the operator enters the seven-digit circulation number, whether or not it is a special edition or from the reserve collection, and the borrower's number.

The other transactions are handled only with an authority badge. They include the "claims returned" procedure which is used when a patron disagrees with the library's claim that a book he has borrowed is still out. The pressing of the correct function key and entry of the book circulation number through the keyboard sets off a search for and flagging of the transaction record. The patron inquiry is similar to the claims returned procedure, except that it is initiated by the patron who receives a printout the next day indicating the books he had checked out.

"Message flag and clear" is a new capability that is especially useful to large libraries where patrons may have inaccurate or outdated name and address records or excessive fines outstanding. The social security numbers for these patrons are flagged so that the next time they seek to make a transaction through an input station, the unit will signal the operator of the action to be taken, including verifying the bearer's identity in the case of a badge reported lost.

The emergency charge procedure permits a patron without a badge to take out a book.

At the end of the day all the transaction information is formatted by the Singer System 10 computer and transferred onto a magnetic tape. It is then processed by the UNIVAC 9300 computer which prepares a master tape to update the master circulation file. In addition, the 9300 prints a wide variety of reports, statistics and documents. These include the first, second, and third overdue notices mailed to delinquent borrowers. If a fourth notice is required, the borrower is automatically billed for the cost of the book plus processing charges. The 9300, incidentally, is also used for the library's acquisition program—a separate system that we will not review here.

In addition to the terminal capabilities, another important consideration in our selection of the Singer data collection system was the unique operational capabilities of the System 10 processor.[4]

The Singer System 10 is distinctively different from other competitive small-scale computer systems in three significant ways: (1) as many as twenty independent jobs can be processed concurrently with multiprogramming controlled by hardware rather than software; (2) a System 10 can be equipped with unusually large amounts of both main and auxiliary storage—up to 110,000 characters of core memory and up to 100 million characters (ten disk drives) of on-line disk pack storage; (3) CRT display units or typewriter-like workstations as well as card readers, punches and printers may be connected to the central processor via simple two-wire lines and can be located at distances of up to 8,000 feet away, or they can be linked to remote locations with a device called a remote terminal scanning system. This is the method used to link outlying terminals, located in other library buildings, to the computer at McKeldin.

The System 10 computer is a very flexible system that can combine batch processing with timesharing operations and also offers multiprogramming.

Generally, a multiprogramming computer system that is capable of concurrently operating a number of independent programs is controlled by a software operating system that is both expensive and wasteful of memory space. However, in the case of Singer System 10 computer, a new approach to the design of multiprogramming systems has been used. Multiprogramming is controlled solely by a hardware operating system which allocates the processor to each memory partition.

The Singer System 10 computer is a fixed partition, multiprogramming computer. Each program is assigned a fixed-size area of main memory referred to as a user partition. Unlike other multiprogramming computers, the System 10 has an area of main memory, referred to as the common partition, or Common, that is shared by all programs in the system. This makes it possible for otherwise independent programs to exchange information at main memory speeds and to share common subroutines.

Common is divided into three areas. The first 300 locations are used by the hardware executive for storing program status information and is protected. Programs may read from it, but may not write into it. The second area of Common is referred to as nonprivileged and is available to all user programs. The third area is accessible only to those user partitions which have been designated with a jumper on the associated I/O channel as privileged partitions. Nonprivileged partitions may not access this area.

Control of the processor by each of the user partitions is hardware monitored through a round-robin, time-slicing priority system. Each partition receives 37.5 milliseconds for execution.

Whatever the total memory capacity, it can be divided into discrete sections or partitions, which may vary in size from 1,000 to 10,000 characters. To each partition is connected an I/O channel capable of handling up to ten terminals.

When the system is installed, plug-in links are inserted in the memory modules to provide the user with the sizes and quantity of partitions required in his specific application. But the positioning of the links can be changed at any time to meet changing data processing demands, until the limit of 110,000 characters or 20 memory partitions is reached.

Every location in main memory is addressable. Each is numbered consecutively within the common partition and within each user partition.

The transfer of data between main memory and peripheral devices is controlled by two types of I/O channels. The File Access Channel is designed to control the high-speed devices, such as disk drives and magnetic tape drives, and the Multi-Terminal Input/Output Channel is designed to control low-speed devices such as card readers, line printers, CRT terminals, and I/O typewriters or workstations.

Unlike the IOCs, the File Access Channel is a shared facility. The devices attached to the FAC are directly accessible to all programs in all partitions. Thus, several user partitions may share the same disk or magnetic tape files.

Unlike other computer systems, peripherals for System 10 need not be located near the central processing unit, but may be distributed as dictated by application requirements.

The arithmetic and control unit controls all the system's activity, including task scheduling, instruction fetch and execution, and manages I/O peripherals. All processor partitions share the processing capabilities of the arithmetic and control unit.

System 10 software consists of two levels of assemblers and RPG compilers, as well as software for communications, business data processing and disk file management.

Automation has really paid off for the McKeldin Library in terms of greater productivity and economy. Since 1966 only one employee has been added to the loan department staff, even though circulation has been increasing at the rate of 20 percent per year. Without our present automated circulation system we would be out of business. There is no way that we could handle our present volume of transactions manually.

Additional benefits have come in the form of new information and services. For example, an employee used to work full time preparing and mailing out overdue notices on a weekly basis. The fourth delinquent notice acts as a bill for the book plus administrative costs. It goes to the university cashier for collection.

Statistics also used to be a problem area. Now we are improving our research data with each successive generation of equipment. The library has been able to better analyze its patronage to determine whether undergraduates, graduate students, or the faculty make heaviest use of its facilities. It was always assumed that graduate students and faculty members were the heaviest users. Thus it came as a distinct surprise when the survey revealed that the undergraduate usage of the library exceeds the combined usage of both graduate students and faculty.

The greater capabilities of the new system will also permit better analysis of which books are being borrowed, when, how often, and by whom. These data help the acquisitions department fill gaps in the library collection. It has already proved invaluable in filling the shelves of the new undergraduate library.

Although our operating expense had increased with each successive generation of equipment, we believe it is in line with the services performed and additional benefits received. Our present five-year lease rate for the Singer System 10 computer and ten terminals is $3,000 per month.

The next step is to convert present batch operation to an on-line, real-time system. This would substantially speed up inquiries for book locations, because borrowers would have immediate answers rather than waiting for the next day's reports.

For an on-line system, we would need to add additional core memory and probably more disk capacity. This would be no problem with the Singer System 10 because core can be added in increments of 10K up to a maximum of 110K, and the computer can operate efficiently with up to 10 disk drives added to the system.

With an on-line system we could also replace the daily printouts with CRT display terminals. To find a particular book, a patron would simply walk up to a display terminal, type in the book's call number and receive an immediate answer on availability and location.

Another application we are investigating is a subsystem for serials checking that would detect missing issues, institute claim procedures, anticipate renewal dates and handle the entire billing procedure. This job of keeping track of 19,000 serials and periodicals is now done manually with a cardex system. We could improve serials service and save labor costs with the addition of a CRT display terminal and/or workstation in the serials department.

We are also considering a library materials budget application that would provide detailed listings on allocation of funds, expenditures, funds remaining by department and category, and funds unencumbered. We have over 100 departments on campus that have yearly book budgets. Better statistics would help each department's library coordinator to make the best use of his yearly library materials allocation by providing up-to-date statistics on purchases of books, serials, and audiovisual aids.

Once one is familiar with the flexibility and multiprogramming capabilities of the Singer System 10 computer, more and more applications come to mind. We have found this terminal-oriented computer system to be particularly adaptable to our needs for data collections at the University of Maryland. We recommend it highly to any library considering an automated circulation system or other data collections projects.

## REFERENCES

1. "Minicomputer Shipments, By Number, To Jump by 50% This Year," *EDP Industry Report*, Nov. 9, 1973, pp. 1-3.

2. Dickinson, R. V., and Orr, W. K. *Systems 10: A New Approach to Multiprogramming*. San Leandro, Calif., Singer Co.

3. Hamner, Walter C. "Credit Card Control Speeds Library Data Flow," *Government Data Systems*, 3:32-41, May/June 1973.

4. The Systems Staff. "System 10: Operations Manual." College Park, Md., University of Maryland McKeldin Library, 1973.

LOIS M. KERSHNER
Librarian, Circulation Services Division
The Charles Patterson Van Pelt Library
University of Pennsylvania
Philadelphia, Pennsylvania

# Management Aspects of the Use of the IBM System/7 in Circulation Control

In the fall of 1972, the Van Pelt Library of the University of Pennsylvania Libraries installed the IBM System/7-2790 Data Communication System for circulation control replacing an IBM 1030 Data Collection System which had displaced a manual system in 1969. This article will describe the System/7 installation at the University of Pennsylvania with emphasis on the management aspects of the system with only brief mention of circulation procedures or processing programs. Reference will be made to variations in S/7 implementation by six other libraries.

## System Configuration Description

The University of Pennsylvania Libraries, with a collection of 2,473,000 volumes, serves a student body of 20,000 and a faculty of 1,730. Of the twenty-three libraries on campus, four use the System/7 for circulation control: the Van Pelt Library, housing the general book collection of 1,455,000 volumes in the humanities and social sciences; the Fine Arts Library with 55,000 volumes; the Wharton School of Business Library with 163,000 volumes; and the Penniman Education Library with 93,000 volumes. Books are borrowed from these four libraries using a punched identification badge issued by the office of the registrar, and a punched 80-column book card prepared by the library's Data Input Office.

Van Pelt Library, with an annual out-of-library circulation of 170,000 has four 2791 area stations for circulation transaction input, whereas each of the three departmental libraries with a smaller annual circulation of approximately 20,000 has one 2791 area station. These seven terminals are connected by a single-shielded multiple twisted-pair wire "loop" which leads out from and back to the System/7 minicomputer located in the Van Pelt Library.

The 14K System/7 supports the 2791 area stations; a 5028 operator station; the S/7 data files; and S/7 programs used for file initialization, file load from and transfer to the System/370, data capture from the 2791 area stations, and transaction logging on the fixed S/7 disk. The circulation control software packages for the System/7 used were developed by IBM with the University of Pennsylvania and are available from IBM as Field Developed Programs.

Communication with the host computer uses a binary synchronous adaptor, 2000 BPS Modem, voice grade line, and 2703 Transmission Control Unit Port. Transmission is at 2000bps via a dial-up facility, with processing on a System 370 Model 168 using OS/VS2 operating system at UNI-COLL, a computer consortium serving a number of colleges and universities in the Philadelphia area.

## Reasons for Selection of System/7

After a thorough study of five circulation systems, initial arguments for a change to the System/7 from a 1030 system reflect an ongoing interest in the management and operation of the system, i.e., factors affecting cost and performance. System/7, we argued, with minimal increase in costs, would give increased hardware capability, would increase reliability and decrease maintenance with the less mechanical/more electronic hardware elements, would increase staff productivity by making work easier and faster, particularly with the keyed variable data entry, and would require a minimal adaptation of existing library software and circulation procedures.

## 2791 Area Stations

The programmed transactions of the 2791 area stations is the most important factor influencing staff performance, and consequently staff salary — the most costly component of the circulation budget. The 2791 terminals at the University of Pennsylvania accept twenty-four transactions, of which five (with asterisks) are not currently used. The major transactions are:

Charge
Discharge
Renewal

Reserve Discharge
Fine Paid: Fine Paid Entry*
    Fine Paid Renewal
    Fine Paid Discharge
    Fine Paid Entry, Keyed*
Call-in Request

Two transactions, Keyed Transactions and Special Transactions, are broken into several components by keying a function code. These are:

Charge, Keyed
Borrower's List
Borrower's List, Keyed
Reserve Charge, Keyed
Call-in Request, Keyed
Card Data Entry
Badge Data Entry*
Keyed Data Entry
Restricted Patron Entry
Delete Call-in Request
Change Reserve Period
Sign On*
Sign Off*
Badge Check

The 2791 area stations accept punched card, punched badge, and keyed data. This ability to key numeric information allows great flexibility in data entry for borrower identification numbers, loan periods, access numbers (or accession numbers), or codes.

All keyed data are easily verified before entry of the transaction by checking its display in a panel on the front of the terminal. A mistake noticed in the display may be cleared and correctly rekeyed without causing an error.

The terminal operator is guided through each step of a transaction by means of lighted messages on the Operator Guidance Panel. This panel matrix of thirty-two messages saves much time in the training of new staff members, particularly at the beginning of a new semester when up to as many as thirty new student assistants arrive in one week to work not only during the daytime hours when a supervisor is available, but also late nights and weekends when a supervisor is usually not on duty. The instructions also give guidance to the regular staff member entering transactions used occasionally. For example, to charge a book the messages read "Insert Patron ID," then "Insert Book Card." However, a more complicated transaction, such as entering or deleting a Restricted Patron will have as many as five instruction messages to complete the transaction.

Several terminal transactions such as Restricted Patron Entry or Delete Call-in have built-in safeguards so that they cannot be used except with the express permission of the supervisor. These transactions require a supervisor key to be placed in the terminal in operation-mode before they may be performed, thereby preventing entry or deletion of data by unauthorized persons.

Since the 2791 area station transactions are programmable, a change in the function of a transaction is possible should such a change be necessary after initial planning. At the University of Pennsylvania one and one-half years have passed since we worked on the specifications for the terminal operations. Now that we are adding reserve book circulation to the system, our requirements for the reserve transaction have changed from our original specifications. With the flexibility that the programming capability of the terminal provides, we are able to have reprogrammed, at our expense of course, the Reserve Charge and the Keyed Data transactions to permit great variation in loan period for each library.

## System/7 Files

The on-line file capability of the System/7 is one of the major advantages of the system over both the totally off-line system, which cannot provide immediate response, and the totally on-line system, which requires continuous connection with the main computer. The on-line files, which I will describe individually, are named Access Number, Call Number, Reserve Book, and Restricted Patron. A fifth file, the Transaction File, accepts information on-line but stores the data for later transmission to the host computer which then processes the data.

The Call Number File contains the call numbers and requestor number for books in general circulation which have been requested for use by another patron. As a book is discharged, a check of the Call Number File providing a match aborts the transaction and causes a "hold" message so that the book may be placed on the hold shelf. Upon the charge of a "hold" book the borrower ID number is checked against the file so that the first requestor only may charge the book. If the person charging the book is not the first requestor, the transaction is aborted, and the appropriate message notifies the terminal operator of this condition. Two requestor ID numbers may be held with each call number to provide for two charges of a recalled book in a single day.

The Access Number File contains the computer-assigned sequential access number of books which are called in. Since books are renewed or called in using this 6-digit number, which is listed beside each call number on the circulation printout, a matched entry on a renewal transaction will result in the message that the book has been called in. For books being recalled, display of the number of outstanding requestors will appear on the terminal display panel.

Deletions from both the Access and Call Number Files are made after processing by loading a program on the System/7 to pull back the library program update for each file from the host computer.

The Restricted Patron File contains the ID number and the numeric restricted reason code as entered by the library. A match made with this file as an ID badge is inserted in the terminal, or the ID number is keyed on the terminal, aborts the transaction, lights the appropriate message and displays the reason code. The restriction may be overridden by use of the supervisor key so that a patron restricted by one library might borrow at another as determined by library policy. The reason code contains three digits, two for library code and one for reason, so that more than one library may place a patron on the "restricted" file for a variety of reasons, such as lost ID badge, wrong address, or a large unpaid fine total.

The fourth on-line file, the Reserve Book File, contains the book, borrower ID and reserve loan period information. A discharge will eliminate the record from this file. However at discharge, if the book is overdue, the overdue time in hours and minutes will display so that a fine might be collected. The reserve transaction activity is passed into the fifth file—the Transaction File—for statistical reporting and those listings to be provided by the library processing programs.

The Transaction File, which can presently hold 15,000 transactions, gathers sequentially the input data and notes the julian date, terminal address, transaction code number, and time of each entry.

The ability of the on-line files to detect books which have been called in saved 2.5 hours per day of a library clerk's time by eliminating the necessity to retrieve recalled books from the library stacks and sorting shelves. The ability to detect improper withdrawal of a recalled book has saved the followup created when it was not possible to know in every case if the proper person was charging the book. The immediate knowledge that a book has been called in permits more accurate information at the circulation desk when either renewing or recalling that same book.

The use of the Restricted Patron File to alert a patron that his address has not been updated, to catch an ID badge that has been reported "lost," or to remind the patron with very overdue books or unpaid library fines to rectify that situation has saved time spent in locating a library patron who, prior to using the System/7, could often not be identified at all.

Five months after the System/7 was installed, the Van Pelt circulation staff was able to decrease staff size from ten to nine full-time clerks due directly to the time saved by the on-line file capabilities and the increased speed with which the 2791 terminals accepted transactions, particularly those requiring keyed data. The departmental libraries, however, with less staff, have not been able to decrease staff size because of their need to have sufficient numbers of people to cover circulation desk schedules.

## Factors Affecting Operation

Transmission of the files to the host computer is such that the instructions for start-up and initial program load are short and easily followed by the library staff simply by pressing the Start, Reset and Program Load buttons on the System/7 and typing brief instructions into the 5028 operator station. Thus, no specially trained personnel are required to handle the normal procedures for daily operation. The library clerk on duty in circulation until the library closes at midnight transmits the data as his final responsibility of the day. An average day's file of 3,000 records takes approximately 30 minutes to transmit.

Altogether six programs are utilized regularly by the library staff: SHASP to transmit data to the host; ANINE, CNINE, and TNINE to wipe out the Access, Call Number and Transaction Files after successful library processing is verified; RHASP to receive updated A and C files from the host; and LIBRARY to initiate the S/7 loop. Several variations may be used within the transmission of the Transaction File so that either a totally new file may be sent, or a partial file adding to a previous transmission starting with *Record XXXXX*, or a partial file to be viewed as a new file starting with *NEW* (record) *XXXXX*. These variations enable transmission of records to the host computer at various intervals, without the necessity for successful library processing to occur after each transmission.

When the library wishes to process after transmission of data, a telephone call is made to the university data processing office to enter the circulation job deck on their remote terminal. The library batch processing programs, written in PL/1 by the library systems office, process the transactions and update files usually four nights each week. These programs generate a circulation listing, notices, reports, messages, and punched book cards. The output is transmitted back to the university data processing office for printing, decollating, and bursting before morning delivery to the Van Pelt Library.

The circulation staff can control all of the anticipated circulation operations. By entering a single punched card through the 2791 terminal using the Card Data Transaction, instructions are logged to run the special jobs using library program cataloged procedures producing the "End-of-the-Month" procedure which reorganizes the master file and prints monthly bills, or "Stack Search" request which lists in call number order all active tracers, Reported Lost-Reported Returns, and very overdue books. Job decks are entered at the data processing office to obtain faculty clearance notices, to change a loan period or fine assessment, to add an internal location badge, to change a notice message, or to obtain address lists for students, university personnel or library courtesy borrowers.

The service of a person trained in programming or operations is required for maintenance of the processing programs, or for special listings and reports. With the close of the library systems office in May 1974, the library has a contract with a local software firm to maintain the applications programs.

Maintenance of the hardware and System/7 control programs is handled by IBM as necessary. Loop diagnostic testing is done using 2K of the memory without the need to bring the loop down. Preventative maintenance is aided by the logging of error messages on the 5028 operator station connected to the System/7. Thus, when a particular terminal is losing tolerance for ID badge variations, the appropriate coded message is produced so that the badge reader might be adjusted. The excellent IBM service provided for the 1030 system has proved to be the same for the System/7. Should the loop need to be brought down for special line testing, arrangements are made to do the testing at times convenient for the library. Should the loop go down during normal operation, it is reinitiated by Load Library, a four-statement program, on the System/7 via the 5028 operator station.

## Staff and User Response

The changeover from the 1030 System to the System/7 in Van Pelt Library was accomplished easily because of the similarity in operation of the 1030 and 2791 terminals. Batch program conversion was chiefly in the editing program to allow for the new S/7 record format. For the three departmental libraries, changing from a totally manual system to the S/7, the change was eased by complete documentation by IBM for the system software and by Van Pelt for the circulation software and procedures. Formal instruction by the circulation librarian covering the operation of the terminal and the basic concepts of the library processing was held while equipment was being installed.

After several tests of programs with data input through the System/7 by the Van Pelt staff, the Van Pelt library changed from the 1030 system to the 2791 system in one day. After just one week of parallel operation, the departmental libraries were anxious to stop their manual systems to concentrate on the automated system. With one and one-half years of operation using the System/7, the initial enthusiasm for the system is still evident in the answers to a recent survey.

The staff likes using the terminal, finds it easy to use and faster than the 1030 terminal in acceptance of data. It finds the guidance instruction panel easy to follow, and uses the instruction messages particularly when entering a little-used transaction. Staff members with experience using the 1030 system said that benefits of the System/7 are greater reliability and versatility, less chance for error due to mechanical problems, and the ability of one terminal to handle all transaction types. Those staff members comparing the System/7 to a manual system said that S/7 benefits are that it: eliminates routine overdue searching and tedious recordkeeping, allows more time to assist the library users, provides better organization of the work to be done, enables work to be kept up to date, eliminates illegible charge records, and makes circulation information readily available to the public.

In a recent survey of user response to the new circulation system, 82 percent of the 406 respondents said they like the automated system; 15 percent said they liked it most of the time, while only 2 percent said they disliked it; 91 percent said book charging was faster; and 72 percent said they rarely had to stand in line to get a book charged.

## Reports

Although not a specific function of the System/7, a noteworthy aspect of the management of the circulation system is the reports generated by the library processing programs, such as daily statistical reports, terminal usage, interlibrary loan charging, inventory and missing book listings, and collection usage. Altogether the programs provide for twenty notices printed on mailer forms, and twenty-four messages which can be produced daily as applicable. A History File containing book information, borrower ID, date charged, date discharged, date due and transaction status at time of discharge is used for report generation as requests arise. The addition of the Reserve Book Circulation File will enable us to look at reserve collection usage by call number, length of loan, and time of day.

As part of the recent circulation procedures and user study, a statistical report indicating the number of transaction types per hour per terminal enabled the staff assignment for charging and discharging to be rescheduled on the basis of proven activity. This eliminated 31 hours per week of time previously designated for these functions.

As with most other automated systems, however, the greatest savings have not been with reduction of staff, but with the increased activity and output of the staff. Even with an increase of 10 percent in circulation activity and the decrease of staff size since the installation of the System/7, library clerk assignment to service a very busy information desk has been increased by 6 hours a day, and all functions are now regularly performed including an extensive monthly stack search for missing books.

Occasionally the loop is down so that a backup procedure for charging using a temporary book card set must become operational. However this occurrence is rare, and the invalid format listing for bad transmission of data is so infrequent that several months pass before an error of this type is listed for correction.

## Responsibility

Several aspects of the circulation procedures are controlled centrally: the keypunch operation for production of book cards; entry of all card data transactions—tracers, reported returned/lost, and temporary book cards; the dissemination of output; handling of supplies; system maintenance; and system operation. This centralization has provided a channel for clear communication between the four library circulation departments, IBM personnel, and the library systems planning office. However, each library maintains control for its own policy regarding loan periods, fines, exceptions to restrictions, and hours of operation. Each library receives its own circulation listing, messages, notices, and daily reports.

The budget considerations are handled centrally by the Van Pelt circulation department, so that decisions such as to process during premium time, not to process at all, or the proposal to extend and modify the system for reserve circulation are made by the circulation librarian in conjunction with the systems office or in consultation with the director of libraries. Unlike many automation projects, the library is totally responsible for the cost of supplies, equipment, maintenance contracts and processing charges at UNI-COLL where processing is done during the third shift to keep costs at a minimum. Costs of the DPC for paper, printing, decollating and bursting, however, are assumed by the DPC and are not currently charged to the library.

## Uses of System/7 by Other Libraries

Although I have described the use of the System/7-2790 data communication system as used by the University of Pennsylvania, other libraries using the System/7 for circulation have made modifications in the Field Developed Programs, or contracted separately with IBM to write support for the System/7 to meet their specifications. Brookdale Community College utilizes the keyed data function heavily for charging of nonbook materials by modifying the charge transaction of the FDP. A two-digit media code assigned to audiovisual materials or equipment kits allows up to ninety-nine different types of material to circulate by keying the assigned number in the terminal.

American University, Georgetown University, Howard University, and the University of Ottawa collaborated in the development of their system requirements. Each uses fewer transactions on the 2791 area stations than the FDP provides, and each uses three files on the S/7 disk—Transaction, Hold, and Delinquent Patron. At American University two 1053 printers are attached to the area stations for the printing of fine receipts upon entry of the Fine Paid transaction. Georgetown uses a printer for receipts, exit passes, and brief messages, for example to flag a hold book or an ID being used with no address on file. Georgetown can inquire the Transaction or "Log" file via the 5028 printer. Both universities have the host computer call up the System/7 for the transmission of data.

The University of Ottawa, with an asynchronous communication link to a 360/65 computer, has developed programs to IPL from a remote terminal when transmission of data from a S/7 disk to the computer needs to be initiated.

Slippery Rock State College uses a System/7 without a disk which connects directly to the school's 370 computer or to an 029 keypunch when the computer cannot be dedicated to the library.

White Plains Public Library, with needs differing from college and university libraries, is using six transactions—charge, discharge, renewal, special loan, reserve or "hold," and update for reserve and patron alert updates. Their processing will be handled somewhat differently by removing the S/7 disk and taking it to the City of White Plains data processing center, there using a compatible IBM System/3 computer for processing. Inventory control will be handled by attaching a 2796 terminal to the System/7 loop. This terminal will be taken to the stacks where the book card accession number will be read into the terminal and registered in the System/7 disk file. A match of these items against the circulation file and bibliographic file will determine the missing items.

## Future Plans and Summary

The University of Pennsylvania Libraries is successfully using the System/7 in four libraries for main stack circulation control. Plans to extend the use of the system to the reserve book collection are well underway. To do this a second disk will be added to the System/7 and core increased to 16K. Since developmental efforts will no longer be borne by the library in the form of a library systems staff, the library has contracted with IBM to modify System/7 software to enable use of the disk and with Information Engineering to modify the library processing programs to manipulate a reserve file for report purposes.

The circulation system using the System/7 minicomputer, or a distributed logic computer system, has the advantages of: immediate detection of book reservations; on-line file search, for reserve collection circulation or restricted borrower; access to recent transaction file on the minicomputer; programmable transactions to meet individual library needs; and complete documentation to support the software package for System/7. The on-line features are all available at avoidance of expense of continuous computer time and storage dedicated to the library. Certainly the adaptability of the System/7 to library circulation systems makes it an attractive contender for circulation control.

## Costs

Although the costs of any system vary depending on the configuration of the hardware, the software capability and the algorithm for computer processing charges, the list of costs for the University of Pennsylvania give some information, not for comparative purposes, but for additional information regarding this particular system. Table 1 gives cost information.

Installation of System/7
   Ship terminals                                   $    251.26
   Install terminals–University of Pennsylvania     164.37
   Install terminals–IBM           1,605.93
   Wiring        2,945.26
   Install security/Cate     369.85
   Install data set     115.00
     Total     $5,451.67

Purchase
   4-drawer file for 80-col. cards     99.00
   8-drawer file for bills     155.20
   Wright line card punch     935.00
   Square hole registration punch     475.00
     Total     $ 1,664.20

Supplies
   Book cards         75,000/yr.     137.00
   Temporary book card sets     25,000/yr.     655.00
   Data mailers        75,000/yr.    2,254.50
   Validation stickers     33,000/yr.     330.00
   ID courtesy badges     3,000/yr.     490.00
   (Printout paper–not charged to library)
     Total     $ 3,866.50

Equipment Rental
   Data set       $    79.15/mo.     949.80/yr.
   3 029 card punches     265.00     3,180.00
   7 2791 terminals     1,014.00    12,168.00
   System/7 modules     1,916.00    22,992.00
   1 5028 station     120.00     1,440.00

Program Rental (2 years only)
   Sys/7 control programs     $  275.00/mo.    3,300.00/yr.
   Sys/7 S370 Communications     50.00     600.00
     Total     $44,629.80

Processing*
   CPU, core, storage, channel, cards read, cards punched,     $16,732.00
   lines printed, tape rental, cards, forms change

Staff
   3 data input clerks     23,400.00
   135 clerical supporting staff (inc. 3 supervisors)    138,940.00
   Student assistants–Van Pelt 8072 hr/yr.     16,940.00
                          -3 departmental libraries     ?

*1974 Processing Charges to date are 50 percent less than 1973 charges.

**Table 1. 1973 Circulation Costs for Van Pelt, Fine Arts,
Lippincott and Penniman Libraries of the University of Pennsylvania**

DENNIS N. BEAUMONT
Chairman
Computer Library Services, Inc.
Newtonville, Massachucetts

# The LIBS 100 System

Libraries in the 1970s find themselves facing major challenges in terms of a need and desire to increase and broaden services in a period of fiscal restriction. Demand for the tax dollar to support social programs as well as demands placed on other governmental and quasi-governmental sources of revenue require the library to fight not only for budget increases but even to maintain its present level of funds. At the same time, costs for material and personnel are steadily increasing. In order to balance expenses within the budget, libraries must review the allocation of personnel, particularly those used for behind-the-scenes activities. They must question the need for the methods used and the results achieved by many of the functions which have been performed over the years. Among the activities requiring repetitive clerical tasks are the routines for acquisition of materials, and those required to maintain records of circulation. Automatic information processing systems can help the library conserve its scarce human resources and assist in freeing financial resources for uses other than maintenance of costly behind-the-scenes recordkeeping. This in turn allows the library to broaden and extend its services to the community within the current operating budget.

As libraries have looked at costs required to prepare a major comprehensive computer system fulfilling all their requirements, the initial investment has appeared prohibitively large. In view of the high initial costs, few libraries have achieved any overall cost reduction as a result of automation.

Computer Library Services, Inc. was formed with a view to the past history of computer applications in the library field and the problems which have been associated with initiating comprehensive systems operated by library personnel. CLSI supplies a complete information processing system—the LIBS 100—geared to the needs of the individual library. This system is delivered ready to use, including the equipment and programming necessary to meet the library's unique requirements. The library need not hire or retain specialists in library data processing applications. Libraries may now automate without major investment in system development or specially trained staff, and without start-up difficulties frequently associated with this process.

The LIBS 100 will support one or more library applications. The capacity of the LIBS 100 system is geared to the task which it is to accomplish. If the library wishes to broaden the range of activities carried out by the system, additional equipment is added to the basic unit, or additional units are added.

The LIBS 100 is specifically tailored to fit the needs of the library. It reduces day-to-day clerical effort by providing new ways to store and retrieve information, eliminates the need for many separate files and allows the library to reallocate its staff to support needed services.

The LIBS 100 has been designed for use by library personnel. CLSI assists the library in educating the staff as to the role of the system in the library's opearations and how it is used to assist the library's professional staff. Training of personnel is carried on when the system is installed. The applications are self-instructional through use of an operator instruction panel. Messages are displayed on it as the operator types in data. The bulk of the training is done automatically by the interaction between the system and the operator.

CLSI offers both preventive and corrective maintenance for the LIBS 100 system. Since the library does not operate on what might be considered normal business hours but must have its system operational during the major part of the 24-hour day, CLSI provides its own maintenance staff for the total system which is delivered to the library.

As a result of a major investment by CLSI, libraries no longer need to "invent the wheel" individually. Proven systems are supplied tailored to the library's individual requirements. Following is an overview of the circulation control system.

The CLSI circulation control application records circulation transactions, accepts and files hold requests, produces patron letters, maintains patron and title data, aids in inventory control, and prints a variety of statistical reports. In short, the system deals with all of those functions which are normally associated with the circulation control function. This application is a part of the LIBS 100 Library Information System, and can be operated either as a single (stand-alone) application or as part of an integrated information processing system.

The main purpose of any circulation control system is to answer the question: "Where can a particular item be found?" Various circulation control systems are more or less effective in answering this question. The better the answer, the greater the range of services which the library can offer. The CLSI system answers this question better than any other system, because one can find out immediately whether there are any copies of a title which are not checked out, and if they are all in circulation, when they are due to be returned.

While it is possible to imagine manual filing systems which could provide this facility, they would be extremely expensive and cumbersome for any but the smallest library. The LIBS 100 can provide this service simply and economically because of the advanced methods used for entering, filing, and retrieving information about an item.

The on-line design of the CLSI circulation control application is based on providing the best possible answer at the lowest cost practical. When one examines the operations of a circulation control system, it is apparent that some activities occur very frequently, or on a regular schedule, while others are less frequent or irregular. The volume of even the most regular activities varies considerably among the branches in a multibranch library. Certain materials have special problems associated with them.

All of these factors have been taken into account in the design of the CLSI circulation control application. The objective of the system is to control the circulation of cataloged, monographic print material. Any item which behaves like an ordinary book can be handled by the system. There are additional, simplified features which allow the library to circulate other materials such as pamphlets, periodicals, and uncataloged books within the system without difficulty, but with correspondingly reduced information.

Fast, accurate data entry is a fundamental requirement for any repetitious, high-volume activity. This is the basic reason why photocharging and embossed patron card systems are popular. The effort required to record the information is very low, while the accuracy is high. The CLSI bar-encoded labels provide another fast, accurate method of recording the transaction coupled with rapid, effortless filing (a characteristic of photocharging but not of the usual embossed patron card methods) and easy retrieval (a facility available in a limited form in manual filing systems, but completely absent in the photocharging systems).

Broadly speaking, the system is concerned with item and patron identification; a checkout transaction establishes a connection between an item and a patron; a check-in removes the connection. These activities can be performed simply by reading bar-encoded labels with the special light pen. The information is then filed automatically. Additional information such as the status of the patron or the existence of a hold, which is known to the system, is used during checkout or check-in to change the ordinary flow of the activity when necessary. Certain types of statistics are also gathered automatically by the system.

Sometimes it is necessary to do special processing when a book is being checked out, for example, the patron may be delinquent. In these cases, the type of transaction requires more information than that which appears on the label, and the system will be communicating more information than can be handled in a simple illuminated panel display. In this case, keyboard data entry and alphabetic display of responses are required, so the operator must use a keyboard/display terminal.

Since any transaction may be completed using a keyboard/display terminal, small branches which cannot justify more than one terminal should have a keyboard/display. Very small branches may be off-line; that is, they may use any of a number of techniques compatible with this system, or use manual data entry of lists of transactions on a keyboard/display terminal at a central point.

Circulation transactions are quickly and accurately recorded, and the information is automatically filed in such a way that other services may be easily performed. These include answering questions about the status of patrons and books, placing holds (reserves), producing patron letters, and trapping delinquent patrons and copies of books on hold (reserve).

In multibranch libraries, the system can determine which branch has a copy of a book which is not checked out, and a staff member may send an appropriate message to that branch requesting it be held or forwarded to the patron's branch. Holds may be placed against books on order, and be filled immediately as the materials arrive. The details of this operation depend on whether the library has a LIBS 100 book acquisition system and on the means of communication between the two systems.

Patron letters are produced automatically for a number of purposes. When a book on hold (reserve) is returned, a notice is issued to the patron. Overdues and bills are automatically produced. The library may send out recall reminders for books.

The system also produces a number of reports. These fall into several categories: (1) daily reports, which contain, for example, a record of unusual occurrences and a list of titles with many requests against them; (2) operational reports, such as terminal statistics and clearance reports used to verify the accuracy of information about missing items; and (3) statistical reports to meet internal management and legal requirements.

CLSI equipment and services bring to the library all the benefits of modern data processing techniques and all the advantages of an in-house system, without the high cost of establishing and maintaining a specialized data processing staff. CLSI works closely with the staff of the library to insure that the installed system truly reflects the needs of that particular library.

In the following sections, the system functions and options are described. The discussion begins with a description of the library-oriented data recorded by the system and the methods for entering and updating this information. It then proceeds through the normal functions performed by the light pen, the special functions performed using the keyboard/display terminals, patron letters, reporting, and housekeeping functions.

## Circulation Data Base

The collection of information available to the circulation control application is called the Circulation Data Base. Various functions such as check-in and checkout automatically change the contents of the data base. Other operations, such as a patron change of address will also change the contents of the data base.

The following terms will be used frequently in the description of the data base:

1. File—a collection of all records of a single type. For example, all of the patron records constitute the patron file.
2. Record—an organized set of related pieces of information which are usually processed together. For example, the information which describes a patron constitutes the patron record.
3. Field—a defined component of a record, for example, the patron name within the patron record. Usually the fields are the smallest meaningful elements within a record.

The data base is described below in terms of four logical files: patron file—the information about each patron; title file—the information about each title; in-circulation file—records current transactions; hold file—contains outstanding hold requests. The patron and title information, therefore, describe the users and contents of the library, and the in-circulation and hold files describe current activity. In the following discussion, the fields in these records are defined. There are two classes of fields, maintainable and automatic. The maintainable fields are those data items which can be changed directly by an operator. Automatic fields may be examined, but are changed only as a consequence of some other activity of the system. In the tables below, maintainable fields will be marked (M) and automatic fields (A).

## PATRON FILE

The patron data are defined in table 1. When a new patron registers, a record is added to the file containing the basic information required by the library. This would include all maintainable fields except delinquency information. Any of the fields in table 1 may be examined by the operator at any time, even though the automatic fields may not be directly modified.

In some cases, particularly in college and university libraries, the patron information is available from another source in machine-readable form. When this is the case, and the LIBS 100 has the necessary special equipment (industry-compatible magnetic tape, for example), the patron file can be automatically entered or maintained using this data base. The records will be fixed length, and each shall contain the patron name, address, telephone number, alternate key, category, and statistical category. Each of these fields will be fixed length, and will contain blanks if the information is unknown. All fields will replace those in the patron record identified by the alternate key. A new record will be created if there is no record with this key.

The patron file contains a relatively large amount of static information; furthermore, many of the records in the file are rarely referenced (patrons who occasionally or never use the library). The library may wish to place such inactive records on historic files (off-line) and keep only a very limited amount of information immediately available (on-line). The off-line data is recalled to on-line status automatically when a patron becomes active.

The on-line maintenance and inquiry functions relate to active patrons only. A patron is considered active who (1) has a book out or a current hold (reserve) request, (2) has had recent activity, or (3) owes a fine. Since the modification and inquiry functions may only be performed on active patrons, the library would like to keep as many on-line as reasonable. On-line storage is, however, significantly more expensive. With this in mind, the library should select an activity period (time since last activity) which keeps the on-line files as full as practical, consistent with the demands of other files for space. CLSI will help the library establish this date, and will provide methods for monitoring the file sizes.

Off-line maintenance functions include storing, recalling, and purging information. Inactive patrons are stored automatically; a limited amount of information is kept on-line for these patrons (see table 2). Whenever an inactive patron checks out a book, renews his card, or places a hold, his record will be automatically recalled.

| *Field* | *Comments* |
|---------|-----------|
| Name (M) | Up to 25 characters |
| Address (M) | Street, city, state, zip (up to 57 characters) |
| Telephone number (M) | |
| Patron category (M) | On-line library, special reserve room (shelf), on-line branch, off-line library, off-line branch, special (e.g., repair, bindery), disposal, system member. (For individuals, the patron category may be defined by the library so that it determines the patron's loan period) |
| Adult/Young adult/ Juvenile indicator (M) | 1 character, library may choose set of values |
| Last activity date (A) | Month/day/year for checkout, reserve |
| Issuing agency (M) | 3 characters |
| Delinquency information (M) | (Books owed, due dates, amount owed) |
| Alternate key (M) | For access to patron when system assigned patron number is unknown |
| Patron number (M) | Bar-encoded label number |
| Patron status (A) | Delinquent, lost or stolen card, reregistered |
| Statistical field (M) | 1 field used to define statistical category |
| Additional data field (M) | Up to 15 characters of text, e.g., drivers' license number or Gaylord Card number |

**Table 1. Complete Patron Data**

Patron number (A)
Alternate key (A)
Patron status (A)
Patron category (A)
Issuing agency (A)
Statistical field (A)

**Table 2. Inactive Patron Information**

Periodically, patrons who have been inactive for a long time will be removed completely from the system (purged). A patron will be purged after three years of inactivity if he has a clean record (does not owe any fines). Patrons who owe the library a fine will be kept for seven years. All purged information will be printed before it is deleted, if the library wishes.

Certain types of modification have additional effects in the system. Adding or re-registering a patron causes the appropriate statistics to be updated. Lost or stolen card reports require a replacement card with a new system-assigned number to be issued. The old card will be trapped at checkout.

There are two access keys in this system. The patron is automatically identified by the machine-readable patron number on the borrower's card. In addition, there is another key used for inquiry, especially when the system-assigned number is not known. This key should be something which the patron can be expected to know. Normally, CLSI recommends an alphabetic key of nine characters. In university libraries, the campus identification number can serve this purpose. Whenever the patron data base is automatically generated from another source, the identifier must be constructed by that source.

## TITLE FILE

Title maintenance is similar to patron maintenance, but there are some differences because the system must maintain copy identifiers as well as title identifiers. The main functions, therefore, are add, change, list and delete title or copy information, and rename the record.

The fields in a full title record are shown in table 3. An item can be circulated without corresponding title information. Uncataloged material, for example, may be identified simply by the bar-encoded item number. Patron records and late notices for these materials will refer only to the item identification number. It is necessary, however, to include a very limited amount of title information to support the inquiry and hold facilities. These require an association between the item identifier(s) and the separately retrievable title record, since the item identifiers are arbitrary serial numbers, and there is normally no connection between identifiers for different copies of the same work.

The library may choose to identify titles either by alphabetic book-keys or by call numbers (alternate key). In most cases, the book-key approach is superior since fragmentary information can be used to retrieve titles. In some cases, especially in large research libraries, the call number is preferred. CLSI will help the library choose the best retrieval scheme. In libraries using the

The following information is universal (applies to all copies):

| Field | Comments |
|---|---|
| Brief author (M) | 10 characters maximum |
| Brief title (M) | 30 characters maximum |
| Publisher code (M) | 5 characters |
| Edition class (M) | 2 characters (paperback, library, binding, etc.) |
| Edition (other than 1st) (M) | 10 characters |
| Publication (M) | 4 characters |
| Material class (M) | 1 character (record, book, etc.) |
| List price (M) | Maximum list of $320 |
| Call number (M) | The call number can be subdivided into several separately maintainable fields. |
| Date of last activity (A) | |
| Bibliographic reference (M) | LC Card #, ISBN or similar standard identifier |

The following information is available for each volume of multivolume works:

| | |
|---|---|
| Volume number (M) | 6 characters volume description |
| Copy information by volume (M) | See copy information below. |

The following information is on a copy-by-copy basis:

| | |
|---|---|
| Bar-encoded label number (M) | 17 characters |
| Statistical class (M) | |
| No. of times circulated (A) | 3 characters |
| Owning agency (M) | 3 characters |
| Adult/juvenile indicator (M) | 1 character |

**Table 3. Title Information**

CLSI book acquisition application, the keys for title records should be assigned in one place, normally in the order department.

When the library has a CLSI book acquisition application installed, much of the information for the add title function can be obtained in machine-readable form from the book acquisition application. Copy information is obtained in this way. When the author/title information in the title record in the acquisition application is fuller than that needed by the circulation control application, it must be edited to compact it.

The change/delete functions are relatively rarely used. These are performed when a copy is withdrawn, or when it is necessary to replace a label which has been defaced or destroyed. When copies are withdrawn, the title and copy identifiers are placed on the daily log for listing, if the library specifies, along with the reason. Withdrawal reasons are entered in message format by the operator.

The store/recall/purge function of the title maintenance process is also slightly different. A title will be stored off-line when it has been inactive for some time and recalled when it is checked out. This time is adjusted to keep the on-line files as full as practical. This is an automatic function, and takes place during housekeeping operations. The data which are held on-line for stored titles include the bar-encoded label number(s), title key, and statistical category.

The purge operation cannot be performed automatically since weeding requires judgment. The system will produce a list of inactive titles (in shelf order) on demand. The options available are: (1) a list of titles as they are stored automatically; and (2) a list of titles and number of copies each stored prior to a given date and not recalled. These lists are then examined and weeding may be performed selectively. Copies are checked out to disposal using the light pen. If the copy cannot be located, it can be disposed of by keyboard entry.

If a title is added to the file on a temporary basis (i.e., interlibrary loan), it becomes eligible for deletion from the file at the end of the library's specified time period.

## IN-CIRCULATION FILE

This file records the connection between checked-out materials and the patron who has them. The data recorded are shown in table 4. This record is created during checkout. All changes to the in-circulation data occur as a consequence of a library function (check-in, checkout, etc.).

For direct patron checkout:

| | |
|---|---|
| Item identifier (A) | Bar-encoded label number of material |
| Patron identifier (A) | Patron number |
| Date due (A) | |
| Date loaned (A) | |

**Table 4. In-Circulation Record**

## HOLD (RESERVE) FILE

The hold file contains the queue of requests for a title within owning agency. This queue is automatically managed by the hold subsystem and the associated functions. The information recorded is shown in table 5. The data are automatically modified by the hold subsystem and the check-in function.

For each agency:

    Title access key
    Volume number          For multivolume works using
                              same access key

For each hold in queue:
    Date of hold
    Cancel date for hold        If known
    Patron number

For each purchase alert less than 30 days old:
    Date of alert

**Table 5. Hold Information**

## Circulation Transactions

Most of the input to the circulation control application consists of checkout, renewal, and check-in transactions. These may be processed by light pen terminals because all of the information needed may be found on bar-encoded labels. Any of these transactions may be performed at a keyboard/display unit as well. A small branch may have only one terminal; this terminal will be a keyboard/display. Very small branches may have their transactions manually recorded and entered in batches from the keyboard/display at another branch or at the system console.

### LIGHT PEN OPERATIONS

The light pen may be used to record normal checkout and check-in transactions, and certain other transactions. The operator is guided through the various sequences by a set of illuminated lights on the terminal. Whenever the terminal expects input, the enter light will be illuminated, along with another lamp indicating the data type. Whenever data are being processed, the Busy lamp will be lit; while this light is on, the terminal will not accept input.

A normal checkout occurs when the patron has a readable bar-encoded patron card and the patron status is normal, the item has a readable bar-encoded label, and the item is not already checked out. If either the patron or the book has not been converted, the light pen subsystem is used for checkout, but special procedures are followed.

A normal check-in occurs whenever the book has a readable bar-encoded label. The circulation desk clerk sets the terminal function by reading the appropriate bar-encoded tab on the terminal. The function is changed by reading the tab corresponding to the new function.

### LIGHT PEN CHECKOUT

When the terminal is set for checkout (see figure 1), the checkout light is illuminated. A checkout transaction sequence begins when the patron card is inserted in the slot. The light labeled Patron is illuminated.

The clerk then reads the bar-encoded patron ID by drawing the pen across the label. When the label has been successfully read by the terminal, the Enter light goes out and the Busy lamp lights briefly. While it is on, the system checks the patron's status, determining first whether he is known to the system, and then whether he is delinquent. There are four conditions for a patron being trapped at checkout: (1) delinquent—set by system, (2) delinquent—set by operator, (3) lost/stolen card, and (4) outdated card of re-registered borrower. In the latter case, the Exception light goes on, the transaction sequence is terminated automatically, and the operator asks the patron to step over to a keyboard input station where the delinquency is resolved.

If the patron record is clear, the standard Loan Period and Item lamps will light; and the clerk proceeds to read labels affixcd to the books. If a special loan period is required, the clerk reads the appropriate loan period tab before checking out the item. The standard loan period is automatically restored when a new patron is entered. After each item label is read, the Busy lamp lights while the system checks the item's status.

If the item is marked as being in-circulation, the Exception light is illuminated. The operator may proceed in either of the following ways:

1.  Read the Proceed tab on the terminal. This checks in the item from the old checkout and checks it out to this patron. If the item is overdue, the delinquency information is retained and must be cleared manually.
2.  Read the Acknowledge tab on the terminal. The item is not discharged and should be held. Presumably, detailed inquiries about the status of the item will be made shortly, and further actions will be based on the results.

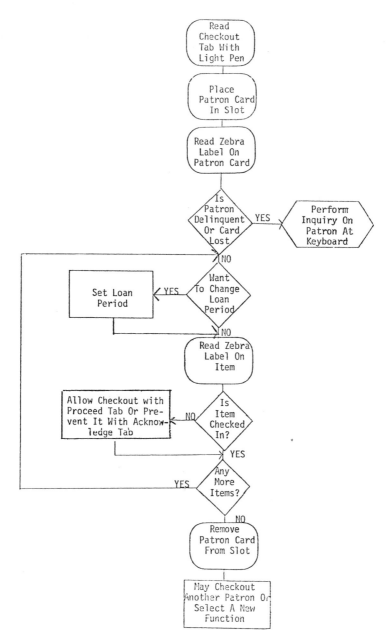

**Fig. 1. Normal Checkout Function (from light pen terminal)**

If the patron and item status are both normal, the checkout is recorded. The relationship between item and patron is noted and the date loaned and due date for the material is recorded. The Loan Period light is illuminated before the book is checked out; the clerk inserts a date slip in the book pocket for the patron's information. The library may choose to indicate due date by another means; CLSI wishes to point out that a reminder of some sort is necessary or at least desirable.

The system displays the Item light after recording the transaction. Any number of books may be checked out in a sequence without re-reading the patron ID. The sequence is terminated by removing the patron card from the slot of the terminal.

Materials may be checked out to other libraries, to repair, or to discard from the light pen terminal. These are treated as patrons by the system, and the circulation desk should have a set of patron cards bearing the appropriate bar-encoded labels for this purpose.

### LIGHT PEN CHECK-IN FUNCTION (SEE FIGURE 2)

When the terminal is set for check-in, the Check-in lamp is illuminated. The Item lamp is also lit. The light pen is drawn across the bar-encoded label for each item. If the label is successfully read, the Busy lamp will light briefly. The system clears the records of the checkout and looks on the hold list for holds against the title. If there are none, the Busy light goes out and the Item lamp is lit again.

If there is a hold recorded for the title, the Hold lamp lights, and the operator may not proceed until the Acknowledge tab has been read. The system notes that the item has been checked in, and a notification will be printed the next time patron letters are produced. The operator places the item on the hold shelf.

When materials which have previously been checked out to an off-line institution (or branch) are checked in, the system records the transactions on the daily log. A report containing these transactions will be printed daily, and the off-line institution may use this report to clear any secondary (paper) records.

### LIGHT PEN CHECK-IN OF OVERDUE MATERIALS

Complete processing of overdue materials is normally performed at a keyboard station. In some cases, however, the light pen is used for these transactions. If the materials have simply been dropped, and the patron is not present, the materials are checked in using the normal check-in procedures.

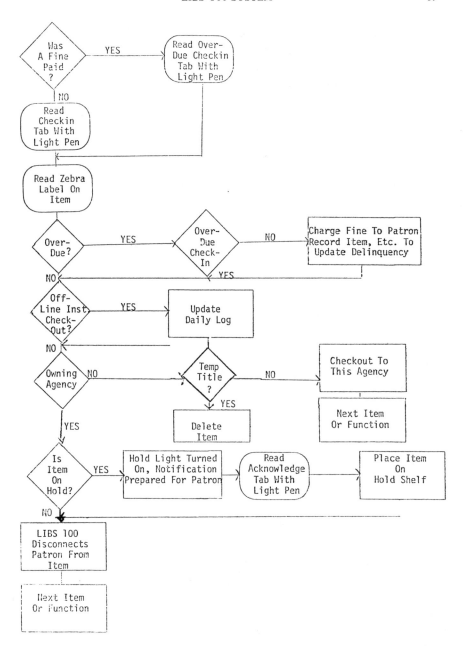

**Fig. 2. Normal Check-in and Overdue Discharge (from light pen terminal)**

The transaction is not, however, cleared, but marked as overdue, returned, the return date recorded, and fine calculated.

If the patron is present, and pays the fine in full, the Overdue Check-in tab is used to clear the transaction and the item checked in. This procedure can only be used for materials in hand.

## LIGHT PEN RENEWALS (SEE FIGURE 3)

The input sequence for renewal is similar to the checkout procedure. The main difference is that the terminal does not remain in Renewal at the end of the transaction sequence. In addition, certain materials may not be renewed. If an item is on Hold or Overdue the Exception lamp is illuminated. The operator must respond by reading the Acknowledge tab. The item is not renewed, and the patron should be so informed.

The date due calculation is based on the date of renewal, not on the original due date.

## LIGHT PEN FUNCTION SELECTION

In general, the various functions are selected by reading a tab on the terminal. Changing from one function to another is accomplished by reading another tab. The following conditions must be satisfied to change from one function to another: (1) The terminal function may be changed at any time during check-in; (2) The terminal function may be changed only between transaction sequences for checkout and renewal operations (no patron card in the slot).

## KEYBOARD/DISPLAY OPERATIONS

The keyboard/display unit is more flexible than the light pen, since the information to be entered need not be pre-printed in bar-encoded form. Most of the more complex functions performed at these terminals are discussed in subsequent sections. The keyboard/display may be used for any normal circulation transaction; in addition, it is used for exceptional transactions including: checkout or renewal to a patron who does not have his patron card with him; mail renewal of materials; checkout of materials to a delinquent patron; handling fines for delinquent patrons; checkout of materials (for example, summer or vacation loan items) for periods other than the established loan periods; and checkout or check-in of an item with an illegible label.

Often it is necessary to identify a patron or a title, or both, to perform these functions or make inquiries. The easiest way to make an identification is

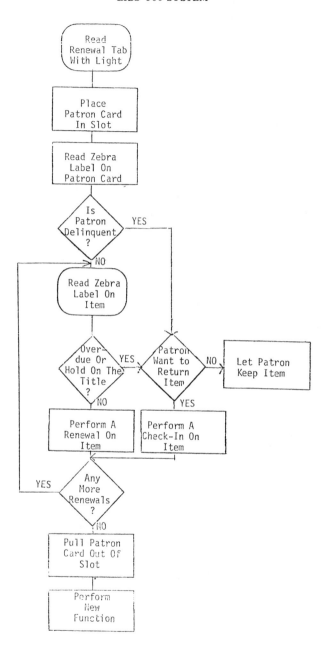

**Fig. 3. Renewal Function (from light pen terminal)**

through the bar-encoded label or the eye-readable number associated with it. If this information is not available, the item or person can be identified by searching the files. The operator enters the title or patron key and the system responds with the record which has that key. This process sometimes results in several possible identifications, and the terminal operator chooses the proper record.

## SAFEGUARD PROCEDURES

The ease with which materials may be checked in or out using the light pen, and the fact that the terminals are in relatively exposed locations on the circulation desk require that reasonable precautions be taken. Any terminal may be shut down by reading the Off tab; the system will not accept messages from it until it has been logically reattached by the circulation desk support system.

Whenever an item is checked in on or before the end of the grace period, the transaction record is deleted. This assures the patron that there is no permanent record of his loan habits. On the other hand, it does mean that the materials checked in can be checked out to the same patron immediately. Reasonable care in handling the materials at the circulation desk will prevent this from happening.

## Hold (Reserves)

The Hold Subsystem (see figure 4) is conversational, and any keyboard/ display, including the system console, may be used to place a hold (reserve).

The first step in placing a hold is patron identification. The operator enters the system assigned patron number. If the patron is a registered user of the library, the LIBS 100 checks his status. The operator may then place the hold or not, as library policy dictates.

The next step is to identify the title. Access to titles is through the Title key. When access to titles is through the Title key, the terminal operator enters the first seven characters of the key and the system responds with the brief author/title which it has recorded for the books which have this partial key. In most cases, there will be one or two titles listed. The full key, including uniqueness digits, is also displayed. There are search facilities which may be used to identify the title when the patron's information is fragmentary (no author, partial title, etc.). While these methods are helpful, the more complete and accurate the information provided, the faster the search.

When the exact title has been identified, the terminal operator may request the due date information for it. The system then displays the due date

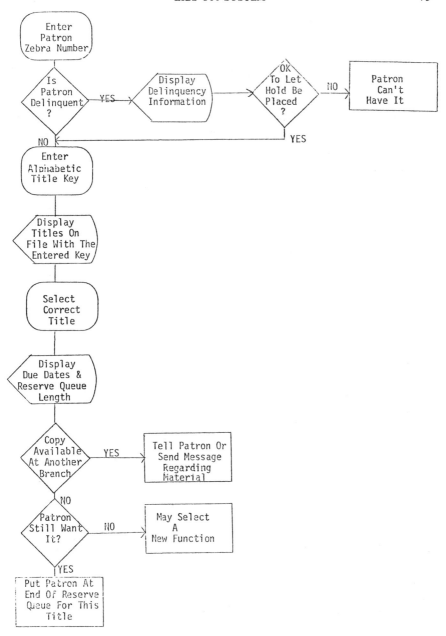

**Fig. 4. Placing Hold Request (From Keyboard/Display Terminal)**

(or due dates if the library has more than one copy) and the length of the hold queue (how many people have already placed holds). In a library that has one or more branches on-line, the copy information includes the owning branch. If two or more libraries share a data base the information initially displayed is that for the library in which the requesting terminal is located. The operator may request information about the holdings of other libraries, if necessary. When a copy is not checked out elsewhere, the operator may enter a message to the other library and ask it to hold the item for pickup or ask to have it sent to the patron's local library or branch.

If there is no copy available for immediate checkout, the patron may have his name added to the queue if he wishes. A cancellation date may be included in the request. If there is a copy in circulation which is eligible for recall, the operator may request a recall notice. Holds are placed against all copies belonging to the requesting branch.

The hold file is checked whenever an item is returned. When the title is found on the list, it is trapped and the system removes the top patron from the list and causes a patron letter to be generated. In addition, the title is placed on the daily log and a report will be printed for the use of the staff managing the hold shelf. This report will contain titles which are being placed on the hold shelf. The report order will be patron alphabetic key or standard identifier, when this is the alternate key. It will be divided by branch when there is more than one on-line branch.

The copy awaiting pickup will be checked out to the hold shelf for a period selected by the library, and the name of the patron who has been notified will be dropped from the queue. If the patron does not pick up the material, it is once more checked in, and if there are more holds, the next patron on the list will be notified.

When a branch queue for a title reaches a certain length (specified by the library) a Purchase Alert is placed on the daily log. The queue length causing the alert is stated in terms of the number of requests per copy. A title will not appear on the Purchase Alert more frequently than once a month for a specific branch.

Holds may be placed against materials which are on order. If the library already owns copies of the title, the hold is placed in the ordinary manner. When the new copies are received, they will be trapped when they are checked in by the circulation system. Procedures are slightly different for titles which are new to the library. The title information may be entered when the books are ordered, and holds placed against it. When the materials arrive, any corrections to title information should be made and the copies entered. The system will check for requests when the item is checked in by the circulation system. Libraries which use the CLSI book acquisition application may have simplified procedures in this case.

If the library withdraws, or marks as missing, the last copy of a title with outstanding holds, titles are listed on the daily log. The holds are not cancelled. The operator may cancel a hold at any time. To cancel a hold, the patron and title must be identified in a manner similar to that used in placing it.

# Reporting

### DAILY LOG REPORT

The daily log report is produced at the end of business each day. It is subdivided into a number of sections, including: terminal statistics (number of transactions, file errors); purchase alerts for hold materials containing author, title, number of copies owned and on order; materials checked in from off-line branches and libraries; last copy withdrawn messages; hold list (holds trapped today); and overflowed patron fine list.

### PATRON LETTERS

There are a number of occasions when the system produces a letter to a patron (see figure 5). The patron letters may be printed on paper stock or card stock. The paper forms are placed in window envelopes, the card stock forms stapled before mailing. The window envelope must be used for bills, since postal regulations do not allow a request for payment to be made on a postcard.

Patron letter print can be performed at any time; the operator specifies which type of letters are to be printed (late notices, hold notification, recall reminders, bills, or collection notices). When late notices or bills are printed, the system automatically finds the overdue items and prints the notice.

The system may generate first, second, and subsequent notices, and bills for materials not returned. The library chooses how many notices shall precede the bill. Before the bills are printed, the library may want to check the shelves for the missing items. The operator may call for a shelf clearance report to aid in this process. The report is in call number order and contains the author, title, and bar-encoded label number for the missing item.

### PATRON AND CIRCULATION STATISTICS REPORTS

The patron and title records contain information which is used to control statistical reporting. There are a number of reports which may be based on this information.

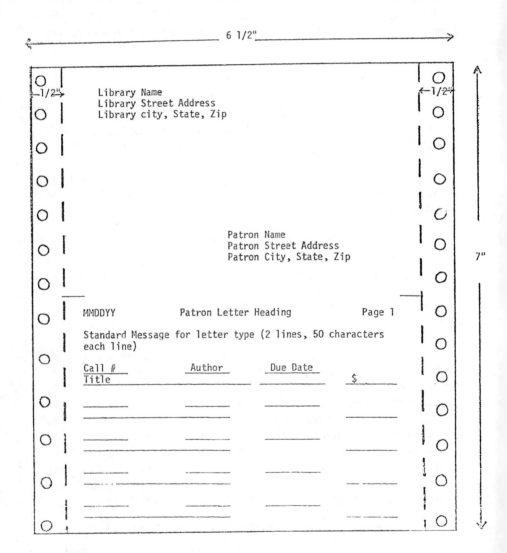

**Fig. 5. Patron Letter**

## Interface with Other CLSI Applications

The LIBS 100 supports a number of applications which may be operated separately, or as part of an integrated information processing system. This section is concerned with some aspects of the relationship between these applications, but is not meant to be an exhaustive discussion of the use of the LIBS 100 in such an integrated information processing system.

There are two types of interface between the circulation control application and other CLSI applications. These may be broadly categorized as direct interfaces, where one application has on-line access to the files of another application, and indirect, where communication is through an intermediate file which may be on-line to both applications but acts as a buffer or letter-box between them. These are not rigid categories, and it may be possible to have direct access for inquiry functions and indirect access for modification.

Under ideal circumstances, direct access would appear to be better since it is more flexible. Rarely, however, are circumstances ideal, and indirect access (or no access at all) is used to protect the files of one application from the activities of another.

The kind of access is also influenced by external factors, such as the corporate relationship between the entities operating the applications and whether the applications share an on-line system resource (disk or communications line). The details of the access type and mechanism are, therefore, not discussed here. The subsections below discuss the kind of information flowing between applications.

### CIRCULATION CONTROL–BOOK ACQUISITION APPLICATION

The main matters of interest in this relationship are (1) the transfer of new title and copy information from the acquisition application, (2) inquiries about materials on order, and (3) the ordering of new copies or titles by the circulation application.

Generally speaking, the amount of information placed in the title file by the book acquisition application exceeds that needed by the circulation control application. Often the former has bibliographic or near bibliographic quality data, while the latter only needs enough to identify an item to an ordinary library user. Therefore, the size of certain fields may be reduced during the transfer.

If all of the titles had been acquired using a LIBS 100, there would be assured consistency between the keys used by the circulation control application and the book acquisition application. Some means must be developed to insure this consistency. The easiest way to do this would be to have all circulation control keys in the acquisition files, or available to the acquisition system. This is not always practical, however; hence there is need for a method of adjusting keys as titles are added to the system.

When key adjustment or further data compression is needed, the records involved will be presented to the operator performing the function. It is strongly recommended that the key produced by the acquisition system be accepted and the conflicting record be renamed. This will reduce future conflicts, since added copies will be automatically appended to the record if it has been produced by the acquisition system.

When the acquisition application and the circulation control application have a direct means of communication, the on-order status of materials can be ascertained at any time. This information is manually maintained in other cases, and is, therefore, less trustworthy.

### CIRCULATION CONTROL–MATERIALS BOOKING APPLICATION

While the characteristics of these two systems are somewhat similar, they differ enough to preclude the use of shared files. There are close connections between the patron activity and when the same patron uses both services as an individual, he may use the same library card. In this case, delinquent status will be checked in both applications whenever the patron is active in either. The patron files may be combined or separate, depending on the requirements of the application implementation.

### INVENTORY CONTROL

The circulation control application will support an inventory control function if the library wishes to convert all of its holdings. Since such a conversion will, at best, take a significant amount of time, manual inventory procedures must be continued. CLSI suggests that the bar-encoded label number be used in place of the conventional accession number for materials added after the installation of the application. If the library continues a second series of accession numbers, manual inventory operations will be significantly more complex, because the reconcilement of missing and in-circulation items requires access by label number.

If the library wishes to do a complete conversion, any systematic approach will work. If the library intends to examine the content of the collection, and to weed extensively during conversion, CLSI suggests that the systematic conversion itself be delayed for perhaps two years so active titles will have been converted before the weeding begins.

The system will construct and maintain a shelflist file to aid in the inventory process. Since this is a bulky, inactive file, it is normally kept off-line. When inventory is in progress, it is recalled a segment at a time. The inventory control terminal (usually a stand-alone recording terminal) is taken to the corresponding shelves, and each label is read. Books with missing or defaced labels are put aside, and the labels replaced. These copies are checked off manually from a keyboard/display. Then the copies on the shelves are checked off and the in-circulation copies are checked off. At the end of this process, any item not checked off is missing. A report containing author, title, and bar-encoded label number, in shelf sequence, is then printed for a final check. Items still missing are then withdrawn.

## Housekeeping Functions

There are a number of housekeeping functions which must be performed regularly in order to keep the system in good running order. These include: (1) daily duplication of files to assure back-up which may be used in case of system failure; (2) weekly patron purge/recall operations which place inactive patrons on the off-line files and restore patrons who have become active to the on-line files; (3) weekly title purge/recall operations which perform similar functions with titles.

During the day, special transaction logging operations are performed to support back-up and maintain statistical fields. This logging is normally done to one of the disk files.

Although this paper has concentrated on its use in circulation control, LIBS 100 is designed to be a flexible, expandable system. The system may be extended to additional library activities by adding further equipment to the basic unit or by incorporating additional units into the overall system configuration.

WAYNE DAVISON
Library Computing Services (BALLOTS Project)
Stanford University
Stanford, California

# Minicomputers and Library Automation: The Stanford Experience

This paper will briefly review Stanford University's library automation system, BALLOTS, and the computing environment in which it is implemented. The system currently utilizes a PDP 11/45 as a communications controller and uses a programmable CRT display terminal. The paper will consider in detail these two current applications of minicomputers and also discuss the proposed use of another minicomputer to support circulation activities. In conclusion, some of the more general considerations and implications of using minicomputers to support library operations will be discussed.

## The BALLOTS System

The BALLOTS system began operation in the fall of 1972. It was conceived and implemented as a full technical processing system for a university research library. As such, it supports all phases of book processing: preorder searching; ordering; claiming and canceling; receipt of material (both ordered items and material received through blanket and approval plans, gifts, exchange, etc.); distribution of material within the library for technical processing and the monitoring and controlling of these books while they are in technical processing areas; and the cataloging of these books and the maintenance of that cataloging data. Bibliographic data in many cases are taken from Stanford's on-line MARC file (supplied by the Library of Congress on weekly tapes). When MARC data are not available, the librarians create records by keying the full bibliographic information at the terminal. It is possible to display these records and review the status of the bibliographic, acquisition, and holdings information. One of the main design criteria for the system was to eliminate redundant keying by capturing bibliographic data once, as early in the process as possible, and then using that data again for printing the outputs, including purchase orders, claim notices, cataloging work slips, catalog cards, spine labels, etc., and for building an on-line catalog.

The heart of the BALLOTS system is the on-line files and associated indexes that provide rapid inquiry and retrieval from the data base (see figure 1). Stanford's file of MARC records now contains approximately 144,000

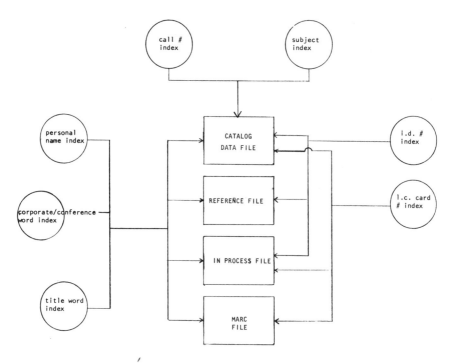

Fig. 1. On-line Files and Indexes

records. The In Process File contains information about material from the time it is ordered until it is cataloged. When material is cataloged, the acquisition data are discarded and the bibliographic and holdings data are automatically transferred to the Catalog Data File. The Reference File contains cross-reference records. The Catalog Data File and the Reference File constitute an on-line catalog of material processed through the system. These three files now contain approximately 35,000 records. The indexes provide access to the files by any combination of personal name, title word(s), and words in corporate or conference headings. These indexes include added entries, subjects, and series entries as well as main entry and title. There are also indexes for LC card number, BALLOTS identification number, and, for cataloged items, call number and subject headings. The Stanford University Libraries will process about 60,000 Roman alphabet titles through BALLOTS this year.

BALLOTS is currently implemented on the IBM System 360 Model 67 computer that serves the academic needs of the Stanford University community. In addition to the normal batch activities on this machine, there is a timesharing system. The systems relevant to this discussion are the timesharing monitor (ORVYL), the terminal executive (MILTEN), the PDP 11 communications controller, and the interactive terminals (see figure 2). BALLOTS runs as a subprocessor under ORVYL, the timesharing monitor developed at Stanford. ORVYL uses the virtual memory capabilities of the 360/67. MILTEN is currently able to connect simultaneously about 125 interactive terminals of various types through both the 3705 and the PDP 11 front-end communications controllers. The PDP 11 supports all the high-speed CRT display terminals. Simple display terminals such as the Tektronix 4023 are supported one to a line, while the intelligent terminals used by BALLOTS are multi-dropped—several terminals share a line. For all operations on campus, the library uses Stanford lines, not telephone company lines, and Stanford built line drivers and multidrop boxes instead of using commercial modems. Stanford also designed and built the hardware interface between the PDP 11 and the 360/67.

## The CRT Display Terminal System

The PDP 11 provides polling, buffering, translation, device transparency, terminal program loading, and some diagnostic capabilities. Whereas the 360/67 can interrupt the PDP 11 whenever the 360/67 has data to send, communication between the terminals and the PDP 11 is done on a polled basis. The PDP 11 continually asks each terminal if it has data to send. If a terminal is not active, the PDP 11 places it in a lower priority status and polls it less often than the active terminals. Once the terminal becomes active, it regains the more frequent polling status. The PDP 11 buffers the transfer of data back and forth between the terminals and the 360/67. In order to save core in the main frame, data can be transferred from the buffers in the PDP 11 directly to memory in the BALLOTS subprocessor within the timesharing monitor. Therefore, as opposed to the implementation of the

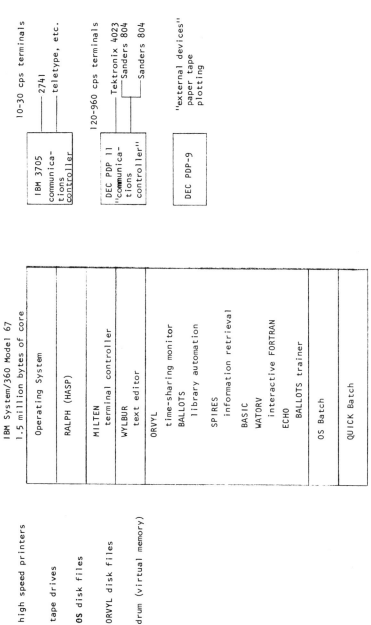

**Fig. 2. Timesharing System**

low-speed typewriter terminals, the PDP 11 implementation does not require buffering within the terminal executive (MILTEN) to handle the data.

The 360/67 sends and receives all data in EBCDIC character code. The PDP 11 does the translation for ASCII character code terminals. The PDP 11 also translates control codes, such as "clear screen" and "home cursor," to fit the particular needs of each terminal. This provides a degree of device transparency to the programs in the 360/67. The PDP 11 contains a copy of the program that runs in the BALLOTS programmable terminals. On request from one of those terminals, the PDP 11 can transmit a fresh copy of the program. This is necessary because the memory in the terminals does not retain the program when the power is turned off. The PDP 11 relieves the 360/67 of the core and programming requirements necessary to support all of these functions. The PDP 11 also supports rudimentary diagnostic and statistical services for the display terminal system.

BALLOTS was the first serious, large-scale application of CRT displays at Stanford. Since BALLOTS provided the major impetus toward the development of a display system, the library's needs played a significant role in the definition of this system. The overall objective was to design a display system that would support the library and other generalized needs for high-speed display terminals. The criteria for this system were: (1) generality, (2) low cost, and (3) high data transfer rates, up to 9600 baud (960 characters/ second). The minicomputer was particularly important in providing the desired generality. It allowed us to define a basic message format for communication with display terminals. This format is used by programs in the 360/67 and then modified by the minicomputer to fit the specific characteristics of each terminal type. Complete device transparency remains a hoped-for but still unattained goal. However, the minicomputer has relieved the 360/67 programs of a great deal of the burden of adapting to specific terminal characteristics.

In order to keep the costs down, we selected the asynchronous mode of communication and decided to poll terminals on a multidropped line. Asynchronous communication is less expensive because it does not require the sophisticated and exact clocking that is necessary for synchronous transmission. The development and maintenance of asynchronous communications software are also less expensive because they are simpler. Multidropping several terminals on each line substantially reduces line costs by reducing the number of lines needed. Since the minicomputer carries on the task of polling the individual terminals on the shared line, the multidrop polling scheme did not place a burden on the 360/67. Stanford further reduced costs by designing and building its own modem replacements and by installing its own communications lines rather than using lines from the telephone company.

The requirement for high data transmission rates came from the characteristics of both the display terminals and the data. Whereas printer terminals send only a single character or a single line of characters at a time, display terminals can send 1,000 to 2,000 characters in a block. Since bibliographic records regularly contain in excess of 500 characters, we could anticipate that BALLOTS would be sending large amounts of data over the communications lines. With several terminals sharing a line it is particularly important to drive them at high speed. When large blocks of data are sent rapidly, rather than individual characters being sent more slowly, there is less contention for the line on the part of the several terminals that are sharing it.

At the time the system was being designed, none of the IBM communications processors could support the breadth of our system requirements. They could not support the variety of terminals nor the transmission rates and communication modes we desired. On the System 360 this is still true, even with the IBM 3705 communications processors. Therefore, the decision was made to use the minicomputer as a front-end communications machine. After conducting a survey, the systems group of the Stanford Computation Center reduced the set of possible small computers to a Data General Super Nova, the Varian Data Machines 620/i, and the Digital Equipment Corporation PDP 11. From the standpoint of reliability, flexibility, and operating characteristics, the PDP 11 appeared to be the best alternative, especially with regard to its flexible busing and I/O schemes. Furthermore, there was already local expertise at Stanford in the installation and use of the PDP 11 as a front-end machine. The PDP 11 is a reasonably fast minicomputer, and the fact that it has byte addressing makes it particularly desirable for text data applications.

## The Programmable Terminal

Since programmable terminals are not yet commonplace, it may be valuable at this point to spend a few moments discussing the structure and characteristics of such terminals. They are small "mini" or "micro" computers. The terminal currently being used by BALLOTS is the Sanders Associates 804 stand-alone programmable terminal. This terminal consists of a bus structure and a small microprocessor. Various devices are attached through registers to the bus (see figure 3). The registers are all 8-bit, or character registers. Some of these registers have stacks and some are devoted to particular devices. The keyboard, for example, is connected via a register to the bus.

A second element in the terminal is the display memory, which drives the display of characters on the face of the CRT itself. The display memory is 8-bit memory and corresponds to the positions on the display. This memory is

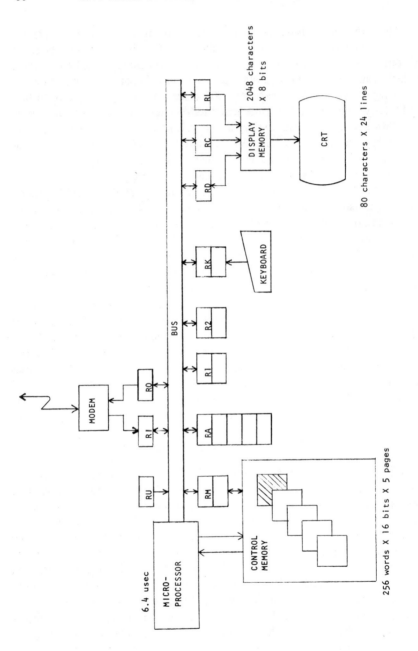

**Fig. 3. Devices Attached to the Bus**

addressable by X/Y coordinates. The modem interface is also connected via registers to the bus.

The program memory, which consists of 16-bit instructions, is accessible through an 8-bit register. To write into or fetch instructions out of the program memory, it is necessary to write the two halves of the instructions separately. The program memory is divided into pages of 256 instructions each.

The microprocessor has a basic instruction set of 16 instructions, although with the various modifications that can be made to those instructions there are effectively 96 combinations available. The microprocessor is also treated as a device on the bus. The microprocessor, of course, has a direct connection into the program memory so that it can execute instructions without their first being passed over the bus. Finally, one of the registers can be used to illuminate status lamps on the front of the terminal.

One page of the program memory is dedicated to a hardwired loader. This is used to receive copies of the program over the modem and load the program into the program memory. Other than this hardwired loader, all the other functions of the terminal are under the control of the program, which was written at Stanford. The program is overseen by an interrupt-driven control program that processes interrupts coming from the modem. This controls the basic I/O functions including error checking and re-try, and supports the polling from the PDP 11. Only a programmable terminal is able to make use of the multidrop˙capability in the display system. The hardwired terminals must each have a dedicated line. The programmable terminals can share lines because the program in the terminal is able to recognize the address of certain messages sent down the line and determine whether those messages are meant for this particular terminal or for some other terminal on the line. The terminal software is also able to interpret various input and output commands, thereby providing greater flexibility.

Finally, the software contains a keyboard-to-display module. When a key is depressed at the keyboard, a character code is deposited into the keyboard register on the bus. The program then looks at the contents of that register and takes whatever action has been coded into the program. The relationship of the keyed characters to the display is completely under the control of the program. This allows tailored editing. The particular functions of cursor movement, the use of tabs, the ability to clear fields, the ability to protect certain portions of the screen, and the ability to expand the format by inserting lines within the middle of the format without disturbing the protected character of the data are all made possible by this programmable capability.

## Designing the User Interface

The main contact a librarian has with BALLOTS is at the display terminal. This is the user interface. Here is where the basic attitudes toward the system are formulated, where user acceptance, and therefore the efficiency of the system, is gained or lost. One of the major activities at the terminal is the input of bibliographic data; and one of our design goals was to make this activity as efficient, understandable, and pleasant as possible. Toward this end it was our decision to use input formats so that, in effect, the librarian would receive a form that could be filled out at the terminal. These formats consistently present individual data elements in the same order, position, and form. Various fields on the formats are tagged and the tags protected. A protected field is an area into which the operator cannot move the cursor and therefore cannot write, change, or erase data. The purpose of a protected field is to preserve system supplied information such as the format of tags and input fields, to reduce the possibility of entering data into the wrong field, and to facilitate the positioning of the cursor for input keying. The cursor can jump automatically from the end of one input field to the beginning of the next. Tab functions can also be used to move forward or backward from field to field.

The most perplexing problem in format design was the wide variation in the length of certain bibliographic data elements. For example, an analysis of 500 personal name main entries taken from MARC tapes showed a minimum length of 6 characters and a maximum length of 53. Ninety percent of the lengths were less than 31 characters. A similar analysis of title statements showed a minimum of 4, a maximum of 919, and a mean length of 40.53 characters. Over 90 percent of the titles examined were less than 75 characters long. Given the finite amount of space available on a CRT screen, it is not efficient to define input fields the size of the maximum length of a widely varying data element. Most of the time a format would be filled with unneeded blanks, fewer data elements could be displayed on each format, and the operator would therefore have to use many more formats to accomplish a given activity.

Our eventual solution to this problem was to provide input fields on the screen for these widely varying data elements that are sufficient to handle the average cases, and can automatically be expanded by the insertion of additional lines to handle those cases where data elements are unusually long. There are many hardwired terminals that allow line insertion and also many that allow the writing of protected formats to the screen. Unfortunately, there are none that provide a combination of both. If a protected format is written out to the screen it is not possible to alter dynamically the length of any of those fields. It was this final consideration that led us to look seriously at programmable terminals that make it possible to have both a protected format and at the same time to have fields that can be automatically expanded as needed. This is possible because the data keyed at a programmable terminal are under the control of the program operating in that terminal, and therefore can be made to behave in any way the program designer wishes.

Working with a programmable terminal was a new and challenging experience. This was particularly true in our case because the first terminal we received was numbered EM01 (engineering model number one). It came with no supporting software other than a very inefficient assembler that ran on the 360. With a hardwired terminal, most of the complex problems of data communications have been addressed by the manufacturer. When one has to write a program to do the same things, one discovers the complex timing problems and error problems in data communications. However, there are also definite advantages to working with a programmable terminal, particularly in debugging. It is possible within the program to stop at various points, look at what is happening to the program, and to step through the program instruction by instruction to find out where the problems are. We wrote a program for one terminal that monitored the data going over the line to another terminal on that same line. We could actually view the data that were going across the line, and see not only the displayable characters, but also the control characters. We could also observe cases where errors were generated.

We used the programmable nature of the machine to build in certain diagnostic capabilities. If the 360/67 is unavailable, the PDP 11 can sense that condition and send a message to the programmable terminal, which will then display the message "SYSTEM UNAVAILABLE." When the 360/67 comes back up, the message "SYSTEM IS READY" appears on the screen so that the operator knows the system is available. In the same way, the programmable terminal itself is able to diagnose whether or not the PDP 11 is alive and well and to present the operator with messages. We use status lamps on the terminal to help the operator be aware of whether or not there are some problems in the line, whether the line is alive and the terminal is being polled, or whether the terminal is still waiting for data to be taken out over the line. All of this is helpful in an environment where people are basically not computer-oriented and do not understand about such things as "start of header" and "end of text" messages, polling characters, and all the other ins and outs of data communications.

Programmable terminals are a specialized member of a growing family of intelligent terminals. All the members of this family are examples of distributed computing, the trend toward decentralized data processing. Some of these terminals still have rather low I.Q. Others rival a large minicomputer in the power and peripheral devices available. The Beehive Super Bee used by the University of Chicago is an example of an intelligent but nonprogrammable terminal. The new IBM 3790 terminals are partially programmable by the user. They allow the user program to deal with the data only at the field level rather than at the character level; and a major portion of the terminal characteristics are contained in the microcode which only the manufacturer can change. The fully programmable terminal is by far the most flexible member of the family. This flexibility was particularly important for Stanford. We wanted to tailor the behavior of the terminal to optimize the library application while also allowing the same terminal to be used for other computing applications. The program currently running in the BALLOTS terminals will behave as a library terminal or as an enhanced 2741 line-by-line terminal. With further development we could load several different programs into the terminal and tailor it to other applications.

When BALLOTS originally decided to use the Sanders 804, it was priced around $5,000. As our needs for memory expanded, and as the terminal was brought out as a market product, the cost has gone up to about $7,500. In the two and one-half years since we began development with this particular terminal, several other programmable terminals have been introduced that can do the same things at more reasonable prices. A $7,500 price tag is more than a library wants or needs to pay for these services. Between now and the end of 1974, we will be conducting another review of terminals. The new terminal will probably be another programmable terminal, but in a clustered rather than a stand-alone configuration. For example, rather than several stand-alone terminals attached to a multidrop box on a line, there will be one cluster of terminals attached to a single line talking to the PDP 11. There will be larger program memory and a larger processor, which will drive a number of displays at one time.

One of the reasons for selecting another terminal is to obtain one that will support the full MARC character-set. We are particularly interested in the programmable terminal with the full MARC character-set that Four Phase may be supplying to the Library of Congress. Programmable terminals are becoming more attractive than they were two years ago. Complete software systems are now available for these terminals. A user can run these software systems without change, or tailor them to his needs without having to develop the entire program from scratch.

## A Circulation System

Thus far we have been discussing the use of minicomputers in library applications that are approximately two years old in their design and implementation at Stanford. As we look into the future, there is at least one additional application where minicomputers will be of value—circulation control. BALLOTS is currently in the process of designing a circulation system; all of the concepts are preliminary and subject to change. We hope to make use of bar-coded labels placed on the inside of the book. These labels will be read by a light pen. Patron identification will be in the form of a punched plastic card. The University of California at Los Angeles has recently issued such a card; and Stanford wants to establish as much compatibility as possible with other circulation systems in California. We hope to install a system that allows self-service checkout. Discharging books, renewal, reserve, overdues, etc., will be handled by the circulation staff.

The In-Circulation File on the minicomputer will contain brief circulation records. This will be a transaction file rather than an inventory file. We will not maintain a permanent circulation record for each of the 3 million-plus books at Stanford. The system will control items only while they are off the shelf, whether in circulation, at the bindery, on interlibrary loan, reserve, etc. The minicomputer will update this file of circulation transactions on-line. The In-Circulation File records will contain an identification number key that will link them to the full bibliographic records stored on the 360/67 (see figure 4). A simple search of the In-Circulation File will be available directly through the circulation minicomputer. It will also be possible to inquire of the circulation system through the BALLOTS indexes on the main computer. When circulation personnel need to inquire of the circulation file they will be able to get basic information from the minicomputer at any time using the piece ID number, even if the large machine is not available. At times when the large machine is available, they will be able to look at displays wherein the minicomputer will not only pick up circulation information from its own files, but will also retrieve the full bibliographic information from the 360/67 files and display a composite record on the screen. In the same way, people working through the main computer using the full BALLOTS indexes will be able to have the BALLOTS program go to the minicomputer, retrieve the circulation status of certain items, and display that information. We will not have redundant data stored in both the main data base and the circulation data base. Printed outputs, such as overdue and recall notices, will be produced in batch mode on the main frame. By the time we implement the circulation system, we hope to be sharing a System/370 Model 158 with the

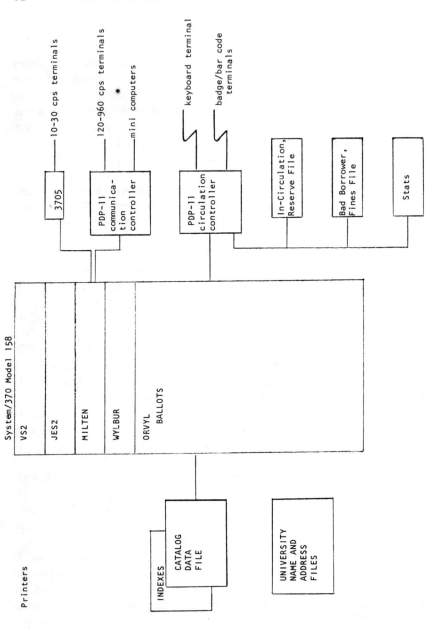

**Fig. 4. System Configuration**

university administrative applications. The batch print programs will retrieve circulation information from the circulation minicomputer, bibliographic information from the Catalog Data File, and patron name and address information from the administrative files.

The main reasons for using the minicomputer in the circulation system are reliability and availability. The library can tolerate 15 minutes of unavailable system time in the technical processing area, and could actually survive a 4-hour lapse on rare occasions. But this sort of system unavailability is simply not acceptable in public service areas, particularly for circulation. The minicomputer is basically more reliable because it is a simpler system. The minicomputer is a simpler machine than the 360 or 370; there is not as much hardware to fail. The software operating in a circulation system like this is also simpler, being single-purpose as opposed to the general, multiple-purpose software on the 360/67. In addition, there are certain times when the 360/67 is just not available; Saturday morning for example. The use of a dedicated minicomputer insures that the library will be able to control the hours the circulation system is available, rather than having to bargain with the general computing community for circulation services.

## Perspectives

One might quite well ask the question: Why didn't Stanford develop the whole system on a minicomputer? The most honest answer is that we developed on the system we had at hand. The 360/67 was available; it already had a timesharing system, a text-editing system, and the beginnings of an information retrieval system. We had people that knew how to program it. It was a familiar environment and therefore the one in which we could do the most rapid development. However, our decision to implement BALLOTS on a large-scale, general-purpose computer was not simply to follow the path of least resistance.

There are three significant issues involved in the choice of computing environment. One is the speed, efficiency, and cost of program development. Compared to a minicomputer, a large-scale general-purpose machine is likely already to provide more of the basic system software and support routines that a library application is going to need; and these programs are likely to be more mature. It will probably be easier to find competent personnel who are already familiar with a large machine. Given the current explosion of interest in minicomputers this situation may be rapidly changing. The minicomputer manufacturers are definitely providing more and better software support for their systems than they did even two years ago. But the leader of a library automation effort must still ask: What is the appropriate development environment for my particular organization, and how compatible will the resulting system be with other systems and other computers? The correct answer will be different for different organizations.

The second issue in general systems versus small dedicated machines is the cost and efficiency of the operations staff. Does the library want the responsibility of actually running the computer itself, of providing space, staff, forms, etc.? Or would the library prefer to contract with someone else for these services? Is it less expensive for the library to go it alone, or to share with others and take advantage of large-scale purchasing power? A dedicated system gives the user maximum control and maximum responsibility.

The third issue is the availability of the library data base to the full community. As libraries develop technical processing systems, they should never lose sight of the fact that the purpose of the library is to serve the patron. By implementing library automation on the general-purpose academic computer, Stanford's bibliographic data are available not only to the library but to the community as a whole. The MARC file and the Catalog Data File produced in BALLOTS are available through Stanford's general information retrieval system (SPIRES) to be searched from any of the 200 terminals on campus. Someone sitting in his physics laboratory, for example, can inquire of the MARC file to see what books have been published recently in a certain area. He can inquire of the Catalog Data File for recent books, to see if the library holds them and where they are shelved. Once the circulation system is implemented, people will also be able to get the circulation status of an item and, perhaps, even make requests for books to be held for them. If the system had been implemented on a stand-alone minicomputer, such data would be unavailable to anyone other than the library itself. Since building, storing, and maintaining the bibliographic data base is the most expensive item in library automation, it only makes sense for as many people as possible to make use of these data.

Another solution to the problem of data base accessibility is a network of minicomputers in which several minicomputers, each serving a different function, could communicate with each other. One processor might be dedicated to library automation, one to information retrieval, one to student use of a language such as BASIC, and another to scientific observation of experiments. Data could be passed from one minicomputer to another, and a terminal could sign into the system and attach itself to whichever minicomputer in the system provided the particular functions and facilities the user desired. As we look towards the future, there are perhaps economic advantages to this kind of distributed computing approach, but that remains to be demonstrated. Stanford is just beginning to do computer network design, so this was not a possibility for us when we began **BALLOTS**. At present we know only a very few successful minicomputer networks. The design of such networks is still very young. Unless someone derives a great deal of satisfaction from being on the leading edge of development and is able to tolerate the expense, frustration, and delays involved, it would be better to wait two or three years before entering this area.

The course of library automation over the next ten years appears to be toward increasing growth of regional networks and the eventual emergence of a national library network. There may be one national system shared by all, or a network of several interconnected systems. In either case, minicomputers and programmable terminals promise to distribute enough computing power directly to each library so that the individual library can maintain compatibility with national systems and at the same time adequately serve its own unique needs.

A. E. NEGUS

INSPEC, The Institution of Electrical Engineers

London, England

# The Application of Minicomputers to Problems of Information Retrieval

Although minicomputers can be used in many types of information retrieval facilities, this paper deals primarily with bibliographic reference retrieval systems. There are two main reasons why it is attractive to consider using a minicomputer for on-line applications: (1) the relatively low cost and (2) the hardware and software provided.

## Definition

It is perhaps appropriate at this stage to consider what is meant by a minicomputer as there is now a considerable overlap in size and capability between the upper end of the minicomputer range and the lower end of many ranges of mainframe machines. Several minis are now available with a memory of 256K bytes and at least one can have a one megabyte memory. Similarly, the range of peripherals that can be handled has grown and it is not uncommon for a mini to handle several 30 megabyte disk drives. All this is far removed from the mini of the mid-1960s which might be equipped with up to 16K of core store and have backing store of one 64K disk plus a tape drive. Another significant change has come in the word sizes used. A few years ago virtually all minis used a 12-bit word whereas now 16-bit words are common, and there is now a minicomputer with a 32-bit word. However, we can identify certain basic attributes that distinguish a mini from mainframe machines. First, there is the price. While a large configuration can be expensive, most minis can be obtained with 16K for less than $20,000 and, perhaps equally important, the store size can be increased by small increments, typically 4K or 8K. Second, they are able to handle a relatively large number of peripherals and often have a capability for many effectively simultaneous I/O transfers facilitated by the hardware techniques employed. Third, a majority of present-day minis are provided with software and hardware that are particularly suitable for real time applications.

This is not meant to be a definitive description of a minicomputer, but it does serve to give some terms of reference for considering the role of minicomputers in information retrieval. Many definitions of minicomputers have been given,[1] and a glance at a list of minis available will show the wide range available and the considerable diversity in size, price and performance.[2] For the rest of this paper I intend to exclude what might perhaps be better described as midis and only deal with machines of up to, say, 128K. After all, there are many IBM 370 installations considerably smaller than a maximum configuration Interdata 7/32 with its 1 megabyte of 32-bit word 750ns store.

## Minicomputers in Information Retrieval

It also seems appropriate to define information retrieval: this paper will deal in general with the retrieval of bibliographic citations, although this will not necessarily exclude the possibility of retrieving abstracts or even full text. In fact this is the area of information retrieval where it is arguably most difficult to employ minicomputers successfully. The problem is, of course, that the size of data bases used will tend to be larger than in many other areas, and its actual size and rate of growth is likely to be unpredictable.

There are two basic types of bibliographic information retrieval: current awareness and retrospective. The first of these, current awareness, can be easily handled on a mini since, whether the products be individual notifications, special interest bulletins or whatever, the amount of material to be handled at any time is relatively restricted. For example, a typical issue of an Inspec tape will contain 5,000 records. In fact minis are rarely used for this type of application, although they are successfully used by the Canadian Defence Scientific Information Service[3] and by the British Food Manufacturing Industries Research Association,[4] who have recently installed a minicomputer to handle all library operations including SDI, other current awareness services and retrospective searches. Minis are probably best suited to continued dedicated use for a task, and most current awareness services are intermittent in nature. Consequently they tend to be run as a batch job on a mainframe machine—either in-house or a bureau machine.

We are then left to consider retrospective searching. For batch searching even a very small mini could be used for searching large data bases provided an overnight turnround could be accepted. For instance, a 12K PDP 8/L with only a 64K disk and one tape deck can search 2,000 or 3,000 Inspec records per minute. Provided one was prepared to swap tapes every five to ten minutes, a search of a data base containing 1 million records could be made overnight. However this does not seem a very promising application and it is in the provision of real-time retrospective searching facilities that minicomputers have an important role to play.

This is not to say that a conventional on-line search package could be successfully implemented on a mini except with a relatively small data base. Nevertheless there are areas where, given a sufficiently large volume of use, a dedicated mini would make economic sense. Certainly a relatively modest configuration could be used with a data base of 50,000 references. For example, the RIOT system at Culham Laboratory,[5] which does run on a large computer, uses less than 40K of store and one 30 megabyte disk pack to provide on-line searches of data base containing 40,000 specially selected references and provides a typical response time of 3-4 seconds with its worst time being 20 seconds. However it is probably true that in most cases where a data base of this size is appropriate, then the traffic on the system is likely to be low, making the provision of a dedicated machine an unnecessary luxury.

An extension of this approach is to use a mini with a recent subset of a large data base which will hopefully answer many queries directly and, for those searchers requiring full retrieval from the whole data base, provide a means by which they can interactively arrive at an optimum search profile which can be used for a subsequent batch search—perhaps overnight on the same hardware. Although some of these possible applications may be valid in certain circumstances, it is probable that the most useful role for minicomputers in a bibliographic retrospective search system is when they are used in conjunction with other hardware. The types of application can be considered in four broad areas: (1) as a front-end preprocessor, (2) in a switching network, (3) as a central facility in a hybrid system using microform, and (4) as a central facility in conjunction with specialized storage devices.

## Front-Ending

Many on-line computing systems use a minicomputer to connect user terminals and perhaps other peripherals to the mainframe. The advantages of this are basically: (1) it removes load from the mainframe by handling such matters as user identification, command syntax and spelling validation and, often, file editing; (2) the operating system on the mainframe consequently need have less facilities—notably much less complicated I/O software can be used, and (3) it is possible to alter the mainframe configuration or even change to a different make of machine without altering the user-image of the system.

Similar advantages can apply to using a mini to front-end a mainframe used for information retrieval. Particularly important is the provision of a stable user-image and the ability to handle a range of terminals that may not only be used with the IR machine and may therefore have varying characteristics. For example, it is desirable that systems should be able to cater for terminals operating in half-duplex and full-duplex as the methods used for suppression of passwords on half-duplex printers (e.g., IBM 2741) are ineffective on Teletype—compatible video terminals and vice-versa. The effectiveness of a front-end mini is such that not only is a much more efficient and usable system provided, but sometimes a financial saving can be made in that the cost of the mainframe can be lower because a smaller configuration can be used.

## Switching Network

In many different areas there is a strong move toward the network concept[6] and, naturally, minicomputers are used for message handling within these networks. Networks arise for a variety of reasons. Some, like SITA, are essentially for message carrying, the purpose being to provide quick, reliable communication facilities at minimum cost.[7] Others, notably ARPA, are aimed at making powerful computing facilities more widely available.[8] Many networks exist, but at present only a relatively small number of information retrieval systems may be accessed via a network. Perhaps the best known example is the National Library of Medicine's MEDLINE which is available over the Tymshare network.[9] However, while TYMNET can handle a variety of terminals operating at a range of speeds, it is still basically a communications network as it merely passes on the message it receives and carries out the necessary code and speed changes.[10] An example of a network provided solely to enable access to an information retrieval facility is that now being proposed by ESRO to provide dial-up access throughout Europe to their RECON service based in Frascati, Rome.[11] Here the remote minis would be able to provide more specific functions and regulate the output to the type of terminal being used.

Perhaps the most valuable application of minis in a network is when they are used to provide access to a range of mainframes all providing on-line search facilities on different data bases.[12] Such a facility (by conversion and buffering of data) would be capable of accepting the many different types of terminal devices actually available to users. It could also provide a simplified standard dialog which would make all the various systems provided look the same to the user, obviating the need for separate training in the use of each different system. It is arguable that systems used with this dialog would be powerful enough to meet most user requests: where a user does not find the information he requires, he would be encouraged to consider making use of the full power of the facilities provided by the system operator and, of course, he would be offered the opportunity of using the original dialog as soon as he had selected a data base.

The principal advantages of this sort of information retrieval network may be summarized as follows:

1.  It allows the user to access several retrieval systems using only one terminal—whatever that terminal may be.
2.  It increases the potential audience for on-line systems—particularly when access is possible over the TELEX network.
3.  It gives the user the option of searching several data bases. If selection of multiple data bases for searching can be achieved automatically the system will, in effect, be offering one large, integrated data base. This may well be a simpler solution when attempted at retrieval time, rather than if an attempt is made to create an integrated data base.
4.  All the retrieval systems made available may be accessed using the *same* stable user image. (A possibility is that future retrieval systems could be developed more easily as the designer could, by initially designing for users of the network, delay implementing a special user dialog.)
5.  It makes central accounting possible.
6.  By using remote multiplexing, considerable savings can be made in line costs.

## Microform Systems

There are a number of factors which have a major influence on the cost and usability of an on-line retrieval system. Three of these are: (1) storage of information within the system, (2) transmission of information to the user, and (3) display of information in an acceptable and attractive form. A technology is now emerging which shows potential as a means of mitigating the effect of these factors. Microforms have been in use in libraries for many years, but it is only recently that the possibility of selecting and displaying frames under computer control has become a reality.

The most widely known terminal is the Image Systems CARD terminal which holds 750 conventional fiche. This has been used in several bibliographic retrieval systems, notably by Intrex and by CID in Luxembourg. Other terminals employing higher reductions (150X) are the Microform Data Systems Terminal which holds 50 ultrastrips, each containing 2,000 A4 page images, and the Automated Microform Terminal now under development by the Marconi Company.[13] This will hold 150 ultrafiche, each containing 3000 A4 page images. At Inspec (with support from the Office for Scientific and Technical Information) we have been evaluating at Marconi AMT and find that storing 6000 A5 pages, each containing a complete citation with abstract, gives a very acceptable display. The user's query is formulated on a Teletype connected to a PDP 8 which carries out the searching. However, the full text is not stored on the computer and on finding a match in the search file the appropriate coordinates are transmitted to the AMT which displays the frame virtually instantaneously. (The delay is less than 1 second when moving about a single fiche and is expected to be typically 4 seconds, with the worst case being about 8 seconds with the 150 fiche magazine.)

At the U.S. Patent Office in Washington, D.C., a system to enable remote access to a data base showing classifications assigned to particular specifications uses MDS terminals connected to a minicomputer, but this is not a bibliographic retrieval system in the sense used throughout this paper.

By using a microimage terminal, the amount of storage needed on the computer can be drastically reduced.[14] By storing dialog and instructional material on fiche the amount of information to be transmitted to the user at any time can be reduced to a minimum, which implies that a simpler I/O package can be used, thus reducing demands on the processor. As the display data are stored on fiche only, index files need be stored on-line. This can, depending on the data base and on the number of different search elements required, lead to the demand for on-line storage being reduced to one-quarter or even one-tenth. This means that a mini can effectively handle a much larger data base in this fashion than it could for a conventional IR system.

## As a Central Facility Connected to Specialized Storage Devices

In the preceding section it was shown how a minicomputer was better able to provide a retrieval facility if some of the processing and storage demands on the central computer could be reduced by using microimage storage.

One of the fundamental attributes of a mini was earlier said to be the ability to handle many separate I/O channels, and it is consequently able to handle a large amount of on-line storage. In fact, the inability of a mini to provide a search system for a large data base is due to the large main memory requirement needed to provide adequate response, rather than to any inherent limitation on the amount of on-line storage that can be handled.

There are a number of reasons why existing on-line retrieval systems, even those using quite large mainframes, are unable to support more than a relatively small number of simultaneous searches, and many of the problems can be overcome to a greater or lesser extent by various means, e.g. front-ending. However, there is one prime factor limiting the overall performance; it is always necessary to transfer a relatively large amount of searchable data from backing store. Various techniques have been put forward and adopted to reduce the amount to be transferred. These range from using novel file structures to data compression techniques and include such ploys as relatively simple partitioning of a data base into subject interest subfields. However, a study of these techniques will show that any reduction in the volume to be transferred is likely to be less than an order of magnitude. The answer to this problem is to devise a system where the amount of searchable data to be transferred is nil; this can be achieved by performing the searching process outside the computer store. Taking the task of searching away from the main computer immediately increases the potential capacity of the system tremendously. Whereas it is unusual for a bibliographic retrieval system to be able to cope with many more than thirty simultaneous users, even with a relatively large and powerful computer, there are many instances in other applications of small machines, even minicomputers, supporting hundreds of terminals or other I/O devices.

During the last few years various articles have described devices, generally described as content addressable, that can separate the searching function from the central computer.[15] A content addressable store can be essentially a conventional disk store (either fixed head or moving head) with local logic for each read/write head. This means that the central computer need only hand over the search statement to the content addressable peripheral which contains the index files, and it will receive back addresses of matching references which can then be retrieved from conventional storage. A considerable amount of main memory that would normally be used either for storing and processing data transferred from disk, or for storing the software to process that data, is therefore released. Consequently, a much smaller main computer can be used or, alternatively, a much more powerful system provided, servicing many more simultaneous users than is normally possible.

It is unlikely that there will be many situations where a mini would be used to support an information retrieval system by itself. However, this is not to say that it does not have a role to play in the provision of retrospective search facilities. The mini is likely to be used in conjunction with other hardware: with a mainframe machine as a front-end, in a network linking users to a variety of mainframes, to drive microimage display terminals, with content addressable stores, or with some combination of these. It seems probable that in most, if not all, retrospective information retrieval facilities of the future minicomputers will be used in one or more of the ways outlined above.

The author would like to thank the Institution of Electrical Engineers for giving permission for the presentation and publication of this paper which represents his own views and not necessarily those of the Institution or of Inspec.

## REFERENCES

1. *Minicomputers: International Computer State of the Art Report* (Infotech State of the Art Report No. 13). Infotech Information Ltd., Maidenhead, Berkshire, England, 1973.

2. "The Minis on the Market," *Computer Weekly*, Minicomputers Supplement:15, Jan. 24, 1974; "Special Report on Small Computers," *Computing Europe*, Feb. 21, 1974, pp. 9-20; and "More About Small Machines," *Computing Europe*, March 21, 1974, pp. 16-17.

3. Irvine, J. J. "A Remote Terminal Retrospective Search Facility Using a Hybrid of Microfilm and Computer Storage," *Information Storage and Retrieval*, 9:597-606, Nov. 1973

4. British Food Manufacturing Industries Research Association, Randalls Road, Leatherhead, Surrey, England.

5. Negus, A. E., and Hall, J. L. "Towards an effective On-Line Reference Retrieval System," *Information Storage and Retrieval*, 7:249-70, Dec. 1971.

6. Greenberger, Martin, *et al.* "Computer and Information Networks," *Science*, 182:29-35, Oct. 5, 1973.

7. Hirsch, Phil. "SITA: Rating a Packet-Switched Network," *Datamation*, 20:60-63, March 1974.

8. Sher, Michael S. "A Case Study in Networking," *Datamation*, 20:56-59, March 1974.

9. McCarn, D. B. "Networks With Emphasis on Planning an On-Line Bibliographic Access System," *Information Storage and Retrieval*, 7:271-79, Dec. 1971.

10. Tymes, La Roy. "TYMNET—A Terminal Oriented Communication Network." In *AFIPS Conference Proceedings. Volume 38. 1971 Spring Joint Computer Conference.* Montvale, N.J., AFIPS Press, 1971, pp. 211-16.

11. Steinacker, I. "Some Implications in Developing a Retrieval Network," *Data Processing*, Aug. 1972, pp. 248-52; Isotta, N. E. C. "International Information Networks: The ESRO System," *Aslib Proceedings*, 24:31-37, Jan. 1972; and Audsley, D. "ESRO's International Space Information Network," *Computer Weekly International*, April 1974, pp. 8-9.

12. Negus, A. E. "ORION Interface—A System for Improving User-Access to On-Line Information Retrieval Systems." Paper presented at the First European Congress on Documentary Systems and Networks, Luxembourg, May 1973.

13. "First Look—Marconi AMT—Automatic Retrieval on Ultrafiches," *Reprographics Quarterly*, 7:24-25, Winter 1973-74.

14. Stern, B. T. "Design Principles for an On-Line Information System Accessing Multiple Files and Using Microfiches—FISHROD," *NCRd Bulletin* 6:158-61, Winter 1972-73.

15. Coulouris, G. F., *et al.* "Towards Content-Addressing in Data Bases," *Computer Journal*, 15:95-98, May 1972; Parker, J. L. "A Logic-Per-Track Retrieval System." *In* C. V. Freiman, ed. *Information Processing 71.* Amsterdam, North-Holland, 1972, pp. 711-16; Clapson, P. J. "Search and Storage Technique for Content Addressable Memories," *IBM Technical Disclosure Bulletin*, 16:1663-64, Oct. 1973; and Ouchi, N. K. "Algorithm and Hardware for Searching on a Key in a Content Addressable Memory," *IBM Technical Disclosure Bulletin*, 16:2217-19, Dec. 1973.

CHARLES T. PAYNE
Systems Development Librarian
University Library
University of Chicago
Chicago, Illinois

# The University of Chicago Library Data Management System

This paper describes the computerized library data system designed and built at the University of Chicago. The project is supported by grants from the Council on Library Resources and the National Endowment for the Humanities and is an extension of an earlier project at Chicago supported by the National Science Foundation. The Chicago system is large and complex, and can be viewed from a number of different aspects, all important to an understanding of the total. The Chicago system is a large data base system; it is also a library data processing system, a data management system, an access system, and a data communication system. It has both hardware and software components, and it makes use of two computers: one large, one small. The University of Chicago Computation Center facility provides the main computing power and data base management. A smaller, front-end computer handles the library's network of forty to fifty terminals and provides a high-speed interface to the Computation Center.

We will look at the Chicago system as a data processing system, as a large data base system, and as a data access system, and also look at the hardware configuration and implementation. First, however, it is appropriate to review briefly the development of the Chicago system.

This is a second-generation project—i.e., one whose staff has had previous experience and has learned the hard way about systems development and implementation. At Chicago, by the late 1960s we had built and were operating a bibliographic data processing system for the library. It allowed data to be input to an in-process file at the time either of ordering or cataloging, accepted input from either MARC tapes or keyboard terminals, and produced printed products for the library. It also produced a large number of machine-readable bibliographic records.[1]

The system has done a lot of production work for the library, handling all Roman-alphabet cataloging and ordering since 1968, and some parts are being incorporated into the new system. The experience with development of this first system, with the operation of it, and with the limitations of it helped shape Chicago's current second-generation project.

In the early part of the current project we undertook extensive work in two areas: (1) to determine and state clearly library data processing requirements, and (2) to develop the computer software capabilities needed to handle library data processing requirements. Most of the exploratory and analytical work is finished and the systems designed. An orderly implementation of the new system is taking place now and will continue through 1974.

## Library Data Processing

Herman Fussler, in a Sloan Foundation report, says that in order to improve information access or costs of library processing operations, changes more basic than simple machine replication of existing routines and processes will be required.[2] Experience at Chicago can add that a data processing system which merely prints products for use in library processing operations does not necessarily improve the way that operation is carried out or even affect the efficiency of it. Clearly, almost all library processing is, in fact, data processing, and as long as library data are processed on slips of paper and maintained and accessed in multiple copies in multiple manual files there will be real limits to the efficiency of the operations. In addition, the larger manual files become, the more difficult the update function is to maintain, and the more difficult current information is to find.

From our analysis at Chicago, the most effective model covering library processing and query operations seems to be one where every operation has immediate access to up-to-date information.

Figure 1 presents a conceptual approach to such a model for library data processing. The essential feature of this model is the central Library Data Base, containing bibliographic and operational data. Assume immediate access to data from all operational points, e.g., selection, circulation, cataloging. Data input is a natural part of the work of each operational point and, once input, the data are, in general, available to all points. Updating becomes an automatic part of most processes, and an update in one operation is an update for everyone. To a very large extent the need for replicating data on multiple

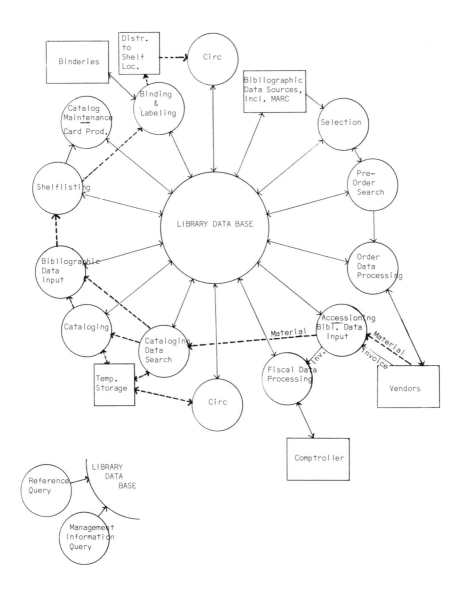

**Fig. 1. Conceptual Model of Library Data Processing**

pieces of paper is eliminated. Ideally, of course, the total of the library's bibliographic and process-related data would be housed in this single data base including everything that is now in the card catalogs. Practically speaking, we are not quite to that point yet, but the rest of this model is realizable and we are thinking about the card catalogs.

The implementation at the University of Chicago follows this model. It makes a significant computerized library data base available to library processing activities through on-line, interactive CRT terminals scattered throughout the library's technical processing, public service, and circulation areas. The system is sized to handle large volumes of data transfer. The CRTs can quickly display screens of data as needed in processing. Each processing operation has on-line access to the data base for querying, searching, and comparing. Each section has the capability and responsibility for input, update, and quality control of its own data. These library data processing capabilities are incorporated in the new system. The structure and composition of the data base and the design of the data base management system will be discussed next, before turning to the system's hardware configuration.

## The Library Data Base

In the Chicago system the Library Data Base is defined as the network of library data—the set of all files of data plus the relations among them.[3] In the examination of library activities and data, the project staff identified those areas where library data are maintained. The Library Data Base includes data about twenty-one such areas, some large, some small:

| | | | | | |
|---|---|---|---|---|---|
| 1. | bibliographic item | 8. | invoice | 15. | seminar room |
| 2. | authority | 9. | fund | 16. | action date |
| 3. | order | 10. | account | 17. | employee |
| 4. | vendor | 11. | loan | 18. | equipment |
| 5. | donor | 12. | patron | 19. | person |
| 6. | binder | 13. | locker | 20. | course |
| 7. | shipment | 14. | study | 21. | department.[4] |

The set of all data for an area comprises a file or files—hence the bibliographic item data file, the order data file, etc. Each file consists of records and records contain data. Data and records may be interrelated, both within a file and among files, and the relationships may be both simple and complex.

Figure 2 presents a simplified, partial picture of the Library Data Base, relating bibliographic data and processing data. The Bibliographic Item File is of central importance in this network of data and is by far the largest file.

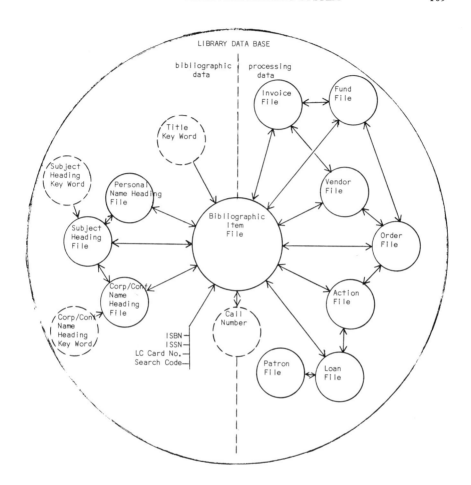

**Fig. 2. Library Data Base**

Each processing data file by itself tends to be rather straightforward and easy to define. Taken together, however, they require a system capability to handle multiple, interrelated files. In these multiple files there is a minimum of redundant data stored. Instead pointers are used to connect data in various files. In almost every case, for example, the processing files are related to and depend upon the Bibliographic Item File for the bibliographic description data. A record in the Order File has an order number, special instructions, and specific volumes, copies, or pieces wanted, etc., plus pointers to the Vendor File, Fund File, Action File (claim date), and Bibliographic Item File. The

Order File also serves as an order number index to the other related files. Pointers work in both directions so that the order record can be reached via the bibliographic item record, fund record, and other related records.

The bibliographic data portion of the data base contains the Bibliographic Item File and the related set of access and authority files and indexes. Bibliographic item records are not stored as a sequence of unit records. Instead, the data structures are designed to provide maximum access capability and at the same time minimum redundancy in storage of data. The Personal Name Heading File, for example, holds the personal name data for the records in the Bibliographic Item File, serves as an index to it, and acts as the personal name heading authority file. Access to the Bibliographic Item File is also enhanced by browsable Call Number and Key Word index files.

In order to display a complete unit record with both bibliographic and processing data it is necessary to pull together data from a number of files. Few retrievals, however, require all data for an item. Also, for common linkages of data, efficient retrieval sometimes requires redundant storage of data. System tuning includes balancing of retrieval needs against data storage costs.

Even within the bibliographic item file itself, the data structures are not simple unit records. Data here are stored in a quadraplanar structure designed to allow multiple users and uses of a common bibliographic data base and yet maintain relationships such as the holdings of an institution or the catalog of a collection, again with a minimum of redundant data. The quadraplanar structure contains four types of planes, or levels, of data, some with multiple occurrences within a given record in the file (see figure 3).

The bibliographic item file structure is designed to accommodate bibliographic records for multiple collections and for either single or multiple institutions per collection. The set of bibliographic records in the file for any one institution may or may not be a catalog—a catalog being defined as a collection under common authority control. Authority control is an option for each collection, and each collection has its own authority control. The data are arrayed so that all collections share data common to all bibliographic records, and so that each collection shares common authority data. Institution-specific data are maintained per institution.

In the quadraplanar structure, the universal plane holds data that are not variable from one copy of a bibliographic item to another. The collection plane, in each instance, holds descriptive data that do not vary within a given catalog and authority structure. (There may be multiple collection planes representing multiple catalogs in the file, however.) Each institution plane holds data that vary between institutions which belong to the same collection. The copy plane holds data that vary with the physical piece.

Data in the Bibliographic Item File are arrayed in the Quadraplanar Bibliographic Item Data Structure. There are four types
of planes in the Quadraplanar Structure. The four types of planes
in the structure and the data present in each plane are:

U, the universal plane - contains data common to all collections;
    includes ISBD(M)data, ISBD(S) data, ISBN, ISSN.

    There is exactly one universal plane in the Quadraplanar
    Bibliographic Item Data Structure.

C, the collection plane - contains data which are collection-dependent
    and common to all institutions contributing to the collection;
    includes entries assigned to the universal data in the process
    of merging an item into a collection--the choice and form of
    entries, e.g., choice and form of main, added, and subject
    entries.

    For N collections $(C_1,...,C_N)$, there are N collection planes
    in the                     Quadraplanar Bibliographic
    Item Data Structure.

I, the institution plane - contains data which are institution-
    dependent and copy-independent; includes call number on
    "cataloging record," local notes, "added" added entries, and
    copy-independent processing data and series decisions.

    For $M_i$ institutions $(I_{i,1},...,I_{i,M_i})$ contributing to collection
    $C_i$, there are $M_i$                 institution planes in
    the Quadraplanar Bibliographic Item Data Structure. The
    total number of institution planes in the structure for N
    collections, M institutions is:

$$M = \sum_{i=1}^{N} M_i.$$

$I^C$, the copy plane - contains copy-dependent data per institution;
    includes call number as on physical piece, and copy-dependent
    data and series decisions.

    There is exactly one copy plane per institution plane in the
    Quadraplanar Bibliographic Item Data Structure; so for M
    institutions there are M copy planes in the file.

**Fig. 3. Quadraplanar Bibliographic Item Data Structure[4]**

    In its initial implementation this data base system will be built and
operated for a single, large university research library with its own bibliographic

and library files. The initial data base at the University of Chicago will consist of Roman-alphabet cataloging since 1968; recent Library of Congress MARC data; partial authority data; and processing data files for circulation, technical processing, and library administration. In regard to processing data, the machine files are intended to replace all manual (paper) files. In regard to bibliographic data, the machine files are designed to include all functions of a true catalog (i.e., control, authorities, and cross references), and replacement of certain departmental and area catalogs is intended as soon as possible. Eventual closing of the general card catalog is foreseen, and this system is designed to replace the catalog.[5]

## Data Base Management System

In order to build, maintain, and access a complex, multifile machine data base there needs to be data base management software. A significant analytical and design effort was carried out by the Chicago project staff to produce the system now installed at Chicago. The resulting system, called HERMES, is outlined in figure 4.

A quality of the HERMES design is its general, as opposed to library-specific, approach to data handling and file management. These basic capabilities are provided by a set of software packages, both commercially supplied and locally developed. HERMES has capabilities designed to meet library requirements and also has capabilities sufficient to meet or exceed the needs of most other large file applications within the university. In its implementation at the Computation Center, the basic data and file handling capabilities of HERMES can be shared with other large file applications on campus, thus broadening the base for support of its maintenance.

A commercial on-line control package handles terminals and input and output of data—converting incoming data to a standard form for the applications programs, handling queues and priorities, and converting outgoing data to a form for transmission. The applications programs are specifically designed for each function, but in general, control data processing.

Chicago Access Support Module (CHASM) controls multiple users, multiple files, and security. It also handles interfile relationships, and in this the CHASM design goes considerably beyond most file management software. In the Chicago system, as noted previously, data base is defined as the set of all files plus the relations among them. The data base management software, therefore, needs to provide capabilities for access to and control of any number of interrelated files. Central control of interfile relations promotes uniform integrity of the data base and also removes responsibility for

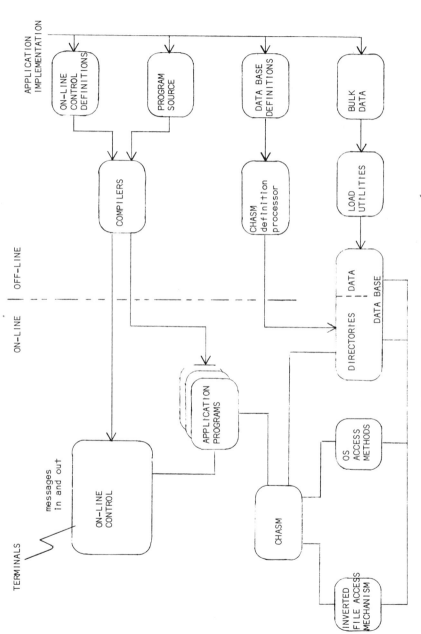

**Fig. 4. HERMES On-line Data Base System[6]**

maintenance of interfile relations from the applications programs. CHASM uses various access methods including a commercially supplied inverted file access mechanism and IBM/OS access methods, including Sequential and Indexed Sequential.

In the overall software design, the relationships of software components are such that applications programs—the programs for specific library operations—are separated from the physical characteristics (speed, character coding, control characters, etc.) of external equipment, such as CRTs, typewriter terminals, and printers, and from the physical aspects of data storage on disks. Separation permits applications to be programmed at a logical data level, which makes coding, testing, and subsequent maintenance and change much easier.

## The Hardware and Communications System

In the early stages of the University of Chicago Library Data Management Project, as the general system design began to emerge, the hardware system design also began to take shape. At first there was no clear requirement for a minicomputer. In fact, it was the university policy that major computing be done at the Computation Center's central facility, and it was also reasonably clear from the beginning that the large data base and data management system would require a large computer for implementation. Later, as detailed library requirements and system design showed the extent to · which on-line interaction was desired and the potential number of terminals needed, the advantages of a minicomputer became more apparent. Data transfer rates and the approximate number of terminals were determined, and a study showed that a minicomputer as part of the front end for the system had definite operational and economic advantages in the Chicago environment. Without a minicomputer, several dozen lines to the Computation Center would be needed. The costs of lines, ports, and modems would offset the costs of a single high-speed line and a small computer in the library. We therefore decided to incorporate a minicomputer front end. A diagram of the hardware and communication system as finally established for implementation of the library data system is shown in figure 5.

The Varian 73 computer in this configuration is not, perhaps, a true front-end processor, at least as defined by John T. M. Pryke, who has described front-end systems for IBM users. Pryke specifies that a front-end processor handles all terminals and connects directly to the IBM selector channel, with appropriate front-end control software.[7] At the University of Chicago, the library is only one of a large number of users of the Computation Center's IBM 370/168 system and did not have this option.

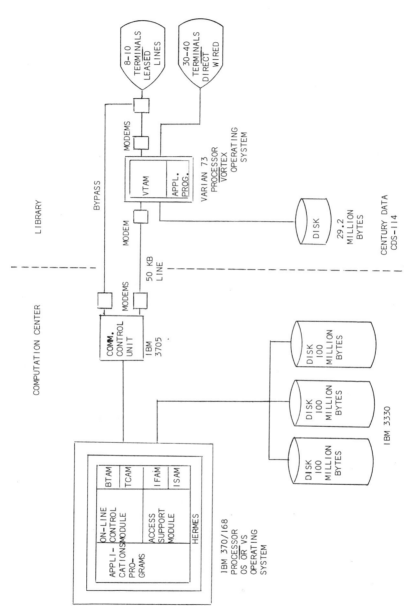

**Fig. 5. Communications and Hardware in Use at University of Chicago**

Instead, the library processor is connected to the channel by an IBM 3705 Communications Control Unit, as are other users. Standard OS telecommunications control programs (BTAM, TCAM) are used.

In this configuration the Varian computer serves principally as a data concentrator and remote multiplexor. It converts data generated by all the various library terminals to look like data generated by IBM 3270 terminals before transmission to the IBM 370/168 facility, which has software established for support of IBM 3270 terminals. The number and type of terminals in the library system are not, therefore, apparent to the main computer.

Any make or design of terminal can be handled through the system with an appropriate program in the Varian 73. This is true of terminals at the University of Chicago and would also be true of terminals not at the University of Chicago, which allows potentially great flexibility in communications with other libraries or network systems. Another advantage of this configuration is that it provides a measure of back-up. If the main computer is down the Varian 73 provides a continuity of service at the terminals. In particular, the circulation function demands uninterrupted service about 18 hours per day. The Varian 73 can, at least, check patron privileges, provide charge evidence, and log data for file updates in the main computer.

Various definitions for minicomputer exist, some suggesting upper limits on the size (or cost) of a machine that can be called a minicomputer. The Varian 73 falls above most such limits, and processors in its range are sometimes called midicomputers rather than minicomputers. Such distinctions are probably not important. What is important is that every machine be of adequate size for its processing requirements. At Chicago, specifications for a front-end computer system were drawn up taking into account projected terminal transactions and data transmission loads, peakload as well as average.[8] Specifications were submitted for bid for a front-end computer system to serve as a data concentrator and high-speed interface to the Computation Center's IBM 370/168. The specifications include the following:

1. processor speed—sufficient to drive the estimated mix of terminals;
2. disk storage—sufficiently large to include software plus certain files;
3. tape drives—two, to log all transactions;
4. console—operator communications and programming tool;
5. communications interfaces—high speed to the Computation Center, a mix of speeds for the terminals;
6. system software—disk oriented, with assemblers or compilers and a communications package; and
7. service—to be locally available and reliable.

Notice that these specifications are not simply for a computer but for a complete system including the communications interfaces.

The specifications were sent to eleven manufacturers and suppliers, and resulted in nine proposals. These responses were evaluated according to the following criteria:

1.  Reputation of manufacturer/supplier—This criterion is the most subjective, but in terms of our requirements, is the most important. The hardware must be widely available and supported over the life of the system, which suggests the importance of dealing with an established vendor. The product must be currently demonstrable and of proven reliability.

2.  Maintenance—Maintenance support must be available locally and should be of proven reliability.

3.  Communications hardware architecture—The major task of the minicomputer system is that of driving approximately forty-eight lines with various transmission characteristics. The communications hardware must be capable of handling a variety of device types and communications characteristics and of processing the anticipated load, and have sufficient reserve power for expansion. Careful attention must be paid to whether the communications hardware controls transmission on a character-by-character basis (programmed I/O) or on a message basis (direct memory access).

4.  Communications software support—In conjunction with the communications hardware, an extremely desirable feature is the availability of communications software.

5.  Peripheral devices—Because the front-end computer system provides back-up when the main computer is down, a heavy burden is placed on the peripheral devices, most notably on the disk drives which hold several processing files. The mechanical components of the system have the least reliability. Therefore, the disk and tape drives proposed must be devices previously installed and of high reliability.

6.  CPU architecture—The state of the art in processor design has reached a point that many fast, reliable minicomputers are on the market. Therefore, CPU to CPU comparisons should be minimized as much as possible.[9]

The Varian proposal was judged best at meeting these criteria and meeting the hardware and software specifications. The Varian system has a 32K Varian 73 CPU. The system has a sixty-four line Data Communications

Multiplexor for all line interfaces and is designed to operate with a throughput of 60,000 characters per second. The DCM is a direct memory access device with a core table for each line on the device providing line dependent information such as buffer address and byte count. The DCM is supported by VTAM, the communications portion of Varian's operating system VORTEX. Various line adapters including synchronous and asynchronous may be tied to the DCM. The character size may be 6, 7, or 8 bit. Parity checking is provided. All lines may be either full- or half-duplex.

## Implementation

The complex, multiple-link communications and hardware system (figure 5) is currently being implemented at the University of Chicago. We can report that such systems do not get into operation overnight. Such systems may require several months to install, to debug, and to test all communications links in all modes of operation.

We are, at one time, testing terminals and programming screens for them; installing communications cables from terminal locations to the Varian site; programming the Varian; testing the data links through the Varian, the modems, the high-speed cable, and the IBM 3705 to the IBM 370/168; enhancing CHASM; developing applications programs; and planning some major file conversions.

It is a busy and difficult period but things are starting to fit. Already some acquisitions and cataloging operations are functioning on-line. The communications system will soon be operational, and the large bibliographic item file (250,000 records) is to be on-line for use by June 1974. By October 1974 the circulation system is to be in operation, and other technical processing applications will be installed by the end of 1974.

Our experience with the development of the University of Chicago Library Data Management System prompts a particular observation. Librarians have done fairly well in the last several years at becoming comfortable with the idea of computers. Computer systems analysts and programmers are fairly common now on library staffs. But another acquaintance probably needs to be made. The University of Chicago system described above is an electronic communication system. Each of the hardware pieces mentioned contains electronic circuitry. Few librarians (and not many more programmers) can read an electronic circuit board, or repair it, or determine the exact point of failure in a system.

Such electronics expertise is needed, and it probably cannot be supplied effectively by service or maintenance representatives of supplier companies. It is difficult for the library to coordinate the technical representatives of four to six different companies when the library does not have the ability to determine whose equipment is at fault. The need for local electronics expertise is even more pronounced if one desires to alter or modify hardware. At the University of Chicago the library has established a working relationship with the staff of the electronics shop of the Enrico Fermi Institute, and their help has proven to be vital to implementation of the library hardware and communications system. We recommend that any library planning to establish any kind of electronic data system try to find an electronics laboratory or shop somewhere nearby and start to get acquainted.

## REFERENCES

1. Chicago. University. Library. *The University of Chicago Library Bibliographic Data Processing System: Documentation and Report as of October 31, 1969.* By Charles T. Payne, *et al.* Chicago, University of Chicago Library, 1970; and —————. *Supplement.* By Charles T. Payne and Robert S. McGee. Chicago, University of Chicago Library, 1973.

2. Fussler, Herman H. *Research Libraries and Technology.* Chicago, University of Chicago Press, 1973, p. 11.

3. Chicago. University. *Library Data Management Project. SuperCHASM Design* (Document no. 87). By Emil Baciu, *et al.* Chicago, University of Chicago Library, 1973, p. 1.

4. —————. *Quadraplanar Bibliographic Item Structure* (Document no. 89). By Jane Jodeit. Chicago, University of Chicago Library, 1973, p. 5.

5. —————. *Library Data Management; Feasibility and Design. Report to the Council on Library Resources and the National Endowment for the Humanities.* Chicago, University of Chicago Library, 1972.

6. —————. *An Introduction to HERMES, An On-Line Data Base Management System* (Document no. 97). By Randall M. Lee. Chicago, University of Chicago Library, 1973, p. 8.

7. Pryke, John T. M. "A Front-End Primer for IBM Users," *Datamation*, 19:46-50, April 1973.

8. Chicago. University. Library Data Management Project. *Specifications for a Front End Computer System and Circulation and Technical Processing Terminals* (Document no. 57). By Randall M. Lee. Chicago, University of Chicago Library, 1972.

9. —————. *Selection of a Front End Computer System for Regenstein Library* (Document no. 70). By Randall M. Lee, *et al.* Chicago, University of Chicago Library, 1973, pp. 6-7.

ANN H. SCHABAS
Assistant Professor
and
GENE A. DAMON
Administrative Assistant
Faculty of Library Science
University of Toronto
Toronto, Canada

# A Role for the Minicomputer
# in Library Education

This paper discusses how one library school, the Faculty of Library Science at the University of Toronto, uses a minicomputer. The pleasures and problems we have experienced with our mini relate to the environment of the school and its educational objectives. They are not necessarily generalizable, but they may provide some insights into the potential of minicomputers. At the outset we should emphasize the newness of our system. We are feeling our way; undoubtedly we are making some mistakes, but we are learning a great deal in the process and are very optimistic about the future. We hope to demonstrate the potential of minicomputers for library education in a way that will be useful for anyone considering a mechanized support system and concerned about the expense and commitment of a large-scale operation.

This paper should be interpreted in the context of our particular situation. Some background on our school, its program, and some description of our environment will make our remarks more meaningful. FLS is old as library schools go. Its forerunners, the Ontario Library School and the University of Toronto School of Library Science, date back to 1928. It has been accredited since 1937. By the mid-1960s it had grown to be one of the largest library schools in North America. It has a reputation for being slightly traditional, but also for turning out students who have solid grounding in the science of librarianship.

If the school is old in years, it feels, to those who are with it now, very young in a number of ways. In the course of the last few years there have been many changes, and some of these have been abrupt and dramatic.

The one-year postgraduate Bachelor of Library Science degree has been replaced by the two-year Master of Library Science as the basic degree. In the old baccalaureate program, the students felt they were on a treadmill. With everything squeezed into eight months, there was little time for in-depth discussion of theory or for research. Only the few students who returned for a further year of study to qualify in the old MLS program had much opportunity to follow areas of individual interest. The switch from a one-year degree to a two-year degree was not made primarily to stretch the time. A totally fresh approach was taken; an entirely new curricular concept was developed. The demand for trained decision-makers, systems planners, and researchers needed to be met. The new curriculum, now in its fourth year, is characterized by the identification of five core areas: the library and its community, resources and collections, organization of materials, library administration, and library research. Basic courses in these areas are taken by all students and a wide range of electives is offered. Each student is free to design the program which best suits his needs and interests. There is an apparent absence of library automation in the above list. Computers, as tools to support library operations, are dealt with in all the core areas. In addition, each student must fulfill a computer programming requirement and may opt to specialize in library automation through the electives he chooses. With this time stretching, there is provision for in-depth study. And the implications of this for an in-house computer facility are great.

The full-time teaching staff has more than quadrupled in number in the past ten years, making specialization possible for individual members of the faculty. Of the twenty-two professors on the full-time staff at present, ten hold doctorates and six others are working toward doctorates. One year ago, official government blessing was given to the new Ph.D. program which had been launched at the school. A recent count identified nineteen faculty and Ph.D. students engaged in research or about to embark on projects.

Last but not least, the school has occupied a magnificent new seven-story building for the past three years. The FLS building is attached, siamese twin fashion, to the new Robarts Library of the University of Toronto which houses the university's research collection in the social sciences and the humanities. The computer-based cataloging project of the newly formed Ontario University Libraries Cooperative System also has its headquarters in the Robarts Library. Occupying two floors of the new FLS building is the FLS library with its specialized collection of 50,000 volumes, a collections budget of about $38,000 and a staff of eleven. The library provides a working model and a laboratory in which we can demonstrate special techniques and approaches for the future librarians who are our students. This model concept has enabled the FLS Library to gain benefits from our automation activities which could not be justified with cost-effective arguments alone.

An integral part of our new building is a full-fledged data processing laboratory with adequate space, atmospheric controls, provision for subfloor wiring and an underfloor cable system throughout the building. This provision for data processing equipment reflects the faculty's philosophy with regard to electronic data processing in library education. The importance of knowledge about automation in libraries is irrefutable. It is safe to say that, with the rapid emergence of bibliographic data bases and cooperative library systems and with decreasing hardware costs bringing mechanization to more and more libraries, the importance of this knowledge for librarians is on the increase.

The positions held by some of our recent graduates bear this out. A number are now systems librarians actively engaged in planning and implementing new mechanized applications in libraries. Others are working more effectively with automated systems because they were able to acquire some skills in this area at FLS. Some now wish they had taken more of the computer-oriented electives. Some older graduates are returning to up-grade their knowledge in this area through the computer electives program. Automation workshops in our continuing education program are one of the high priorities.

Data processing was introduced to the FLS curriculum in 1966. From the beginning, it has been in the hands of library science faculty. This has insured a consistent policy and strong library orientation throughout. An objective then, as now, was to give interested library school students as strong a grounding as possible in computer technology and its library applications, to facilitate good communication with machine people and sound decision-making in this area.

Our first facilities took the form of a crowded, unairconditioned unit record laboratory with keypunch, sorter, collator, document writer and accounting machine, complemented with batch use of an IBM 7094 at the University of Toronto Computer Centre. Automation courses in the baccalaureate program were all optional and minimal—two hours per week of class time for one term including some simpler programming.

In the first year of the new master's degree program, all students complete a set of computer programs—the computer requirement mentioned earlier. This uses a ten-instruction simplified computer, simulated on the university's IBM 370, in batch mode. Our objectives with this assignment are to introduce sequential step methodology in problem-solving, to convey the binary nature of machine decisions, to identify human factors in the man-machine interface, to establish standards for documentation of projects, and to awaken interest and aid the students in identifying their interest in and aptitude for specialization in this area.

Consistent with our hands-on approach are a number of on-line simulations which have been developed as teaching aids for the core courses to familiarize the uninitiated with terminal interaction and to demonstrate the capabilities and sophistication of on-line systems. In particular, we have prototypes of an on-line cataloging system and an on-line information retrieval system. Both CRTs and typewriter terminals are used for these demonstration systems. Also, through the cooperation of the National Science Library of Canada, students have an opportunity to experiment with profile construction for an SDI system.

For students who choose to specialize in the automation area in their second year, we offer a program including studies in documentation techniques, characteristics of information structures, file organization, system design, and information transfer patterns. The six courses fall into two separate but related streams. The documentation stream has a special library orientation and is aimed at the librarian who will be working alone to provide information services to the specialist. The systems stream concentrates on library housekeeping operations, MARC format, file management, and systems design, and is aimed at the librarian who will be planning and implementing large-scale applications as one of a team. All six courses blend theory with practical applications. Most include projects which require programming and other machine interaction.

For the second-year student who has identified a special library problem, the curriculum offers a research stream option which releases him from course responsibilities in order that he may pursue his specific project. Already students working in this stream in nonautomation areas have made good use of computer support services for analysis of data. To date, computers have been used in the doctoral program in a supportive way: for text editing, for statistical analysis of data, and for simulation studies.

We are also building up a first-rate research facility. For this we need a number of things. We need the climate for research, which we have. Our teaching program is research-oriented at both the master's level and the Ph.D. level. Faculty strength in the area of automation and systems has been enhanced by cross appointments from other university departments, including computer science. Staff and staff expertise in information processing and systems are being built up to support a Ph.D. major in the future. A number of faculty are presently engaged in computer-related research and others are using support routines already mentioned. Studies are underway on cataloging practice, indexing effectiveness and thesauri, and using the bibliographic data base of the University of Toronto Library Automation System. To support this research activity, we needed a laboratory, the physical space, and controlled atmosphere for the equipment—and for the people using it. Our new building has provided this. We needed equipment which is sophisticated, up to date, and which provides access to a wide variety of facilities. Variety would insure the flexibility which is so very important in an environment supporting both teaching and research.

It was to support just this philosophy that the FLS undertook, in the period from 1966 to 1970, to develop the functional specifications of computer services for its new quarters. As the 1960s gave way to the 1970s, however, the actual implementation of these specifications differed somewhat from the initial ideas because of changes in the economic climate and in technological developments.

Between 1966 and 1968, the staff of the school—W. J. Kurmey in particular—examined methods for using the computer to the best advantage in the school's program, and these methods were tested, using available equipment in a limited application. With the assistance of other staff on campus, preliminary ideas were developed into a set of requirements. Basically these requirements specified two types of environment: standard batch and complex interactive. Both would have to support the peculiar requirements of bibliographic information storage and retrieval processing (e.g., large data bases, large character-sets and character-string processing, as opposed to straight computational processing), in addition to the general computational functions needed for research, computer-assisted instruction, and administrative processing. It was anticipated that the interactive facility would have a large number of CRT terminals both for teaching and research.

Negotiations with the staff of UTCC and of UTLAS led to the conclusion that neither of these operations could support the projected requirements of the school. While the UTCC facility could provide the general batch services needed by the school, it was not prepared to make the additional resources available for interactive processing. The UTLAS staff, although heavily engaged in interactive processing, did not feel that it could risk the problems resulting from having students and experimental processing in an operational system.

In late 1967 the school, with the help of the UTCC staff and others, developed a proposal for a satellite computer system (see figure 1). The principal function would be to serve as an interface between CRT terminals

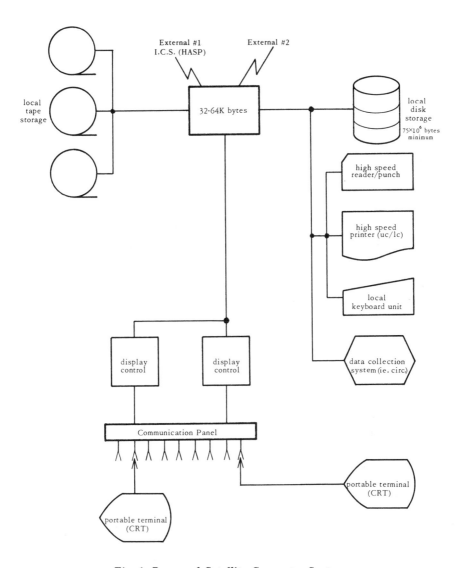

**Fig. 1. Proposed Satellite Computer System**

and the other facilities on campus. In 1967 facilities for a data processing laboratory in the new building were planned using as a model an IBM 360/30 with local disk and tape storage, a high-speed upper/lower case printer and considerable communications equipment. In January 1969 the school received a capital appropriation from the provincial government to be used for the purchase of hardware.

In May-July 1970, with a firm date for occupation of the new building, tenders were received from several computer manufacturers: a Xerox Sigma 5, an IBM 360/30, a UNIVAC 9400, and a RCA SPECTRA 70/35. Although the systems tendered did not meet our specifications completely (or, if they did, were too expensive), the school's committee settled on one of the proposals, accepted the compromises it entailed, and sent its recommendation to the director of the school. By September 1970 the system had been approved by the Technical Subcommittee of the University Computer Policy and Planning Committee. FLS seemed to be on the way to having a medium-sized computer operation.

By 1970, however, a number of things had changed. The most significant was in the economic climate. The school had the capital budget for the equipment, but it did not have the operating budget to support a system such as that being proposed. The university administration, in approving the purchase of the recommended system, would also have to approve an additional annual budget expenditure of between $70,000 and $100,000 for staff and maintenance. They were not prepared to do this, and in late 1970 the school was asked to review its requirements and come up with alternative solutions. In the year and a half that followed, the previous five year's work had to be rethought and, fortunately, other changes occurred which made this easier.

The first of these changes was the decision of the new director of UTCC to provide an interactive service on a large scale. The interactive system that he proposed for the university was an IBM 360/65, separated from the general batch operations on an IBM 370/165, and dedicated to APL, CPS, high-level programming languages, and ATS, a text editing facility. During the early months of 1971, the school experimented with APL. The results showed that although APL was useful for a number of things which we wanted to do, it had serious limitations. In late 1969 and 1970 the school had experimented with CPS and found it to be far from satisfactory. The principal problems of both systems were the file and program size and, with APL in particular, the restriction on the type of terminal that could be used. It was not possible, for example, to use CRT terminals, and there was a severe limit on the size of the character-set which could be processed. APL, as implemented by IBM, was effectively limited to IBM 2741 type terminals. In July 1971, at the suggestion of the UTCC director, a minicomputer was ordered with the software to effect the code conversion needed to interface CRTs to APL. By summer 1972, this system was being used regularly for manipulation under APL of a technical reports file. As a result of this experience, we felt that APL, interfaced through a mini, could be used for some of our processing.

At the same time that the mini was being introduced into the school, there was a change in administration at UTLAS and with it a change of direction in planning for its future. During the months of late 1971, an agreement for shared facilities was worked out between the faculty and the university library. Under this agreement, the faculty purchased major pieces of hardware for use by UTLAS: a CPU, core memory and some peripherals. In return the school was given use of the system, a Xerox Sigma 7 and a Xerox Sigma 6, which, because of the expansion and a new operating system, could support some of the processing the school wished to do. In addition to the normal computer services which this timesharing facility gave the school, there was also access to the Xerox Graphic Printer with its special characters and type fonts.

Most important, however, the agreement has involved the school in a system which is the center of Canada's largest machine-based bibliographic network. It gives the school access to over 15 million records including LC/MARC, BNB/MARC, and Canadian/MARC. In addition, as a spinoff from the basic agreement, the school and the library have jointly developed a special purpose CRT for bibliographic processing.

As a result, FLS became involved with three systems: the IBM 370/165 for general batch, the IBM 360/65 for interactive APL, and the Xerox Sigma 6/7 for other processing, both batch and interactive. This meant that our communication problems were even greater than in the case of the earlier system. Several types of terminals were proposed and planning was underway to use all three systems and often the same data on all of them. By early 1972, we had gained enough experience with the capabilities of the minicomputer and sufficient knowledge about the type of system which our vendor, GEAC Computer Corporation, was designing that in May 1972 we asked them to work with us in designing a system which would meet communications and local processing requirements of the school.

Our present system (figure 2), based on the minicomputer, is functionally not greatly different from the one proposed five years ago—it costs about one-third as much and has several other advantages as well. At present, the maintenance costs for the system are less than $10,000 per year—the staff consists of one student working less than 10 hours per week and about one-third of the administrative assistant's time. One of the major reasons for the low staff costs is that the system was designed as a turn-key system with operator intervention only when serious errors occur or in starting or terminating operations.

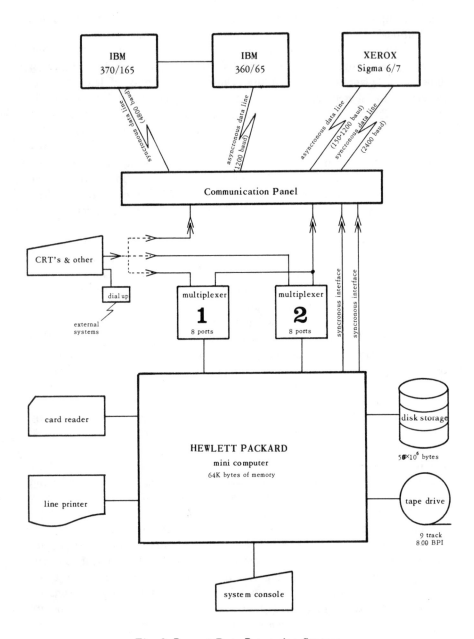

**Fig. 2. Present Data Processing System**

Besides the difference in cost, another advantage of the mini system is that of flexibility in both the hardware and the software. The school's staff had much more control over design of the software than would have been the case in a larger system. At the time of our contract, the vendor was designing an operating system (of which ours is a subset), and we had considerable input into this design. The communication software, designed under our direction, has taken advantage of many local factors which standard package software could not have done. The school also had much more control in the choice of equipment. When considering the tenders for the larger systems, we often felt "Wouldn't it be nice if we could have that printer on this CPU?" With the mini, we were able to make good, cost-performance compromises and buy equipment which we felt could best meet our needs. Thus, we have a Hewlett Packard computer with a CDC disk drive, a Mohawk Data Sciences printer and card reader and several types of terminals—all possible because it is comparatively easy to connect different equipment to the mini.

Inherent in the advantages arising from the flexibility of the system are some disadvantages from the point of view of an educational operation. First, the equipment was bought, assembled and integrated by a middle-man arrangement with the result that it is not a standard system such as we would expect our students to encounter in the field. Secondly, we do not have the stability of a system backed by a large corporation. Finally, we lack the standard language and operating procedures available with a "big name" system. It is felt, however, that these disadvantages are more than compensated for by the mini's flexibility and by the variety of facilities available to our students and faculty.

Having recounted the tortuous path by which the school arrived at its present system and some general statements about its advantages, reasonable questions at this point would be: What does the system consist of in terms of specific software and hardware? How does it work? What can it do? Functionally, the system as it stands has four major components.

## OPERATING SYSTEM

The operating system is a simple one providing the minimum services needed to manage the computer resources in a multiprogram environment. These services include memory allocation, execution control and input/output control. Memory allocation is handled by the loader which brings programs into memory, checks for conflicts of usage, supplies the required information to the system task-control tables and starts execution. A subset of the loader is an executive routine for overlaying program segments and is called from the user program. Execution control is handled by a scheduler which can put a program in any one of six states and uses a priority chain. The six possible states are execution, suspension by a higher priority task, input/output wait, input/output complete wait, executive service wait, and termination processing. Normally a program will execute unless interrupted by a higher priority task, until there is need for input or output. When an I/O request is made, execution is passed to another program. After the I/O request has been satisfied, the program enters the I/O complete wait and will continue execution when the scheduler reaches its position on the priority chain. The executive service wait occurs when the program has requested a system service module which is not presently available, e.g., a call for an overlay. Termination processing is a temporary state during which the system completes the necessary "housekeeping" needed to release a program from the system.

Input/output control is handled by an I/O subsystem which manages requests for I/O devices, calls the appropriate device drivers and processes device interrupts. The I/O device drivers for the line printer, the disk and the multiplexers are integral parts of the operating system. Drivers for other devices can be added to the system or included as part of the application program using standard linkages to the system's I/O controller for interrupt and error processing.

Supporting the system and its use is a general service subsystem which provides access to the software needed to input, test, and debug applications programs and some system utilities such as the file purge routine and file directory listing. From this subsystem the user can access an editor for creating and updating source programs, the assembler and the loader. This service subsystem operates much like a background mode on larger computers but is seen by the system as a large special program. For debugging purposes, programs are run under the control of this subsystem before being added to the inventory of regular programs. Debug aids are in the form of snapshot dumps.

Another of the support subsystems is the spooler, a routine which primarily controls output to the line printer and input from the card reader. It can, however, be used to create a temporary file when passing data from one program to another, when that is necessary and shared access is not desirable.

The languages available on the system are GEAC's version of the Hewlett Packard assembler, Fortran, Basic and OPL, a high-level language designed by GEAC with the capability of having inbedded assembler level instructions in the source program.

## REMOTE COMMUNICATIONS

There are several remote communications modules. Using synchronous communication, the system has direct remote batch connections to both the IBM 370/165 and the Xerox Sigma 6/7 systems. Indirectly through the 370, special batch jobs can be run on the IBM 360/65 for retrieving and storing data in the APL file system. The remote batch facility allows jobs to be transmitted to either of the two machines, allows status inquiry to be made from a CRT terminal and, in the case of the 370, prints the output either on the school's printer or on any of the other remote printers on campus or on the UTCC printers. For the Xerox system, output can be printed either at the school or on the printer at the UTLAS site.

In the planning stage are two more remote communication functions. First, it is planned to provide the capability of intercepting output from one system and rerouting it to another, e.g., data coming back from the 370 could be intercepted and sent to the Sigma 6/7. Thus, for example, new data created under APL on which we have several data entry and edit programs could be off loaded from the APL files and sent to the Xerox system. It is also planned to provide asynchronous communication to the IBM 360/65 to replace the earlier APL interface program and asynchronous communication to the Xerox Sigma 6/7. The objective of the latter software is to allow automatic log-on and provide easy switching from one system to another without the mechanical changes that are presently required. It is felt that this will be especially useful for computer-assisted instruction and research activities where the user is not primarily interested in, or knowledgeable about, the various systems but requires the use of predefined processes such as statistical packages, simulation routines, etc.

Consideration is being given to FLS being a member of OULCS's network with the mini as one drop point on the network. This would give FLS access to the bibliographic system as a regular user. Another possible link which may be considered in the future to enhance the range of facilities would be to the information retrieval systems being established by Canada's national libraries. Should other external systems offer new dimensions, the flexibility of the software and the hardware will make it possible to communicate with them.

## TERMINAL COMMUNICATIONS

At present the system's terminal communications can handle sixteen terminals or terminal-like devices using standard asynchronous protocol. The terminals are handled by two multiplexers which were designed and built by

GEAC and which have the capability of providing various speed and code configurations on each port, i.e., speeds from 110 to 9600 baud and 5-11-bit character codes. In the planning stage is a synchronous, terminal communication subsystem for the special bibliographic terminals.

## FILE SUBSYSTEM

There is a very simple file subsystem which provides the necessary control information for managing source files with the associated relocatable and load module files. The source file part of the subsystem provides blocking and unblocking of the short record which would be created by the editor. The subsystem also provides the control information for user files. These files are made up of contiguous sectors of disk storage which are written or read a sector at a time by requests to the file subsystem. The user is responsible for his own data management routines within the block of disk storage assigned. The system disk, a CDC 9746, provides about 50 million bytes of storage. Since the present system with its various temporary files, source, relocatable, and load module program files, etc. requires only about 5 million bytes of storage, there is plenty of room for local applications and future expansion. Tape files can be created and read in much the same way as tape usage on other systems except that, without an operator, use of tape is limited to users who have been trained to mount and demount tapes. For the present, the tape drive is primarily to be used for back-up and special applications.

As one might guess, the design and implementation of the system which has been described has been a challenge. For the most part, difficulties stemmed from one general problem—lack of experience and available expertise. The vendor, although quite at home with the hardware and other types of applications, was not familiar with library needs or with the school's specific educational objectives. The experience of the school's staff had mainly been with big systems, yet in order to make decisions and provide the information which the vendor required they often had to deal with a level of detail which would not have been true in an off-the-shelf system. Frequently there were delays while the information needed for a decision was acquired. The other units on campus with which we were dealing had little or no experience with this type of application. Because the system is a hybrid of custom software, standard software, and several types and makes of equipment often requiring specially designed hardware, deliveries were quite poor, anywhere from days to months late.

Another significant problem is in the area of documentation. The uniqueness of the system, the fact that the vendor was engaged in several custom systems at the same time and that documentation did not have the highest priority on the vendor's schedule made it a difficult item to get. We had, however, built in an automatic hold-back of payments tied to documentation. The firm is expanding its sales, and good documentation has become vital. In light of this the vendor's priorities have changed, and a full-time technical writer has joined the firm. In addition to the vendor's documentation, there are FLS's procedures manuals and users' guides which must be more extensive than would have been required in a standard system.

Another important problem in a hybrid system such as the school's is maintenance. With such a variety of equipment and special software, trying to establish a set of maintenance arrangements with the different firms could have been a nightmare. However, GEAC is also providing a number of facilities-management operations for users of their systems and has a fairly good maintenance staff. FLS has negotiated a maintenance contract with them. This arrangement will also provide access to changes and enhancements to the basic system as they are developed.

Although there have been frustrations and problems with design and implementation, the results to date seem to indicate that the flexibility obtained and convenience of a fairly powerful in-house system outweigh the problems. Some of these advantages can be seen in the ways that we have begun to use the system.

Presently its most important function is a link between the card reader and the line printer and the university's IBM 370. This gives on-site access to both the HASP job stream and the High Speed Job Stream for batch jobs. We have dedicated disk space at UTCC. On this we continue to build up data bases for administrative, research, and instructional needs. The simulator for the first-year programming problem is stored in this way, as are the files for first- and second-year course assignments and the FLS library's data files. The obvious advantages are convenience and saving of time. Until a year ago, a ten-minute walk across the campus was required, often in inclement weather.

In the spring of 1974 we incorporated the minicomputer as a model in the course on file structures. The circulation system of our own library is being redesigned by the class, hypothetically, to operate on-line using available hardware, principally our data collector and our mini. The university library's Sigma 6/7 will be used for back-up and off-line functions. At the time of writing, this course is still in progress so it is a little premature to evaluate it, but enthusiasm is high among the participants. Within an environment of real constraints, students are gaining experience in systems design, systems development, record and file design, compression coding and hash coding techniques. This approach is making the principles of file organization and information handling gained in the classroom and from the literature much more meaningful.

Not to be overlooked is the usefulness of the mini in providing a local listing capability. This is used by students and staff alike to make listings of programs for debugging and proofreading. Those who are doing calculations of a statistical nature on data stored on punched cards are finding this listing facility invaluable for checking over the data for keypunching errors.

A somewhat novel use of the mini is in operation as a daily notice board, popularly known as the SIN-board (Selective Information Notification). Closed-circuit television screens strategically located in the school's entrance lobby, the FLS Library, and lounge areas flash notices of topical interest. The announcements cycle through at a readable speed, and recycle throughout the day. The texts are stored on the mini, and it is the mini which controls the cycling. Updating may be done as frequently as needed. SIN has implications for library settings where it could serve as a dynamic notice board. In pre-SIN days notices were duplicated and distributed in as many as 300 copies. SIN is living evidence of our fight against paper pollution.

Other applications programs are being developed for the mini. At this point, however, most of the work has been on support software needed for later applications and the expanded communications functions.

The psychological benefits of an in-house system are being realized. The in-house lab helps students to overcome the man-machine interface syndrome so many of them experience at first. With a minimum of direction, students submit their own jobs, tear off their own printouts, and interrogate the central computer for queue status information about their jobs via CRTs. The atmosphere is very informal in our data processing lab, and this encourages a natural curiosity about the relationships between the components, the card reader, the printer, the CRTs, the typewriter terminals, the disk drive and the minicomputer itself. Permanent displays on the walls of the lab to describe the configuration in detail and to explain its relationship to outside systems are planned.

The students have lived through some instances of machine failure. An upsidedown deck in the card reader would jam the printer until software modifications were made to identify and sidestep the mistake. Starting the system up after a software failure is something a number of us, staff and students, can now do with moderate success and considerable satisfaction if and when we succeed. Paper jams on our somewhat temperamental printer are another difficulty we are all learning to deal with. The card reader, too, sometimes balks at swallowing our decks. Students see members of staff coping with these kinds of problems, which contributes to a reduction in the fear of the machine.

The lab is large enough to accommodate a number of work tables and usually these are spread with printouts. Teamwork is encouraged both officially and by the atmosphere. Informal instruction is fostered too. Often one of the heads in a huddle belongs to a teacher.

It is hoped that the future use of the system will bring applications to a more sophisticated level. For research the flexibility of the system and variety of hardware will be able to satisfy individual needs and will provide an opportunity for comparative studies. For students there will be exposure to a variety of alternatives for library applications.

We have already described one class project using the mini. Many other projects suggest themselves for classes in the years to come: taking a different file organization approach to the same circulation system, working on a different subsystem of the FLS library's operation or developing a new service to promote use of available data bases. Developing actual working systems for our library or prototypes of systems gives students an opportunity to observe and evaluate automated systems in action. The systems available for observation should be similar in equipment and sophistication to systems frequently found in modern libraries. Judging from the current thinking of some of the OULCS member libraries, the general pattern for the future will be network tie-in supplemented by an in-house minicomputer. One library in Ontario is already in the process of purchasing a system like ours. Our graduates will go to their future jobs with some minicomputer familiarity. We are not clairvoyants, but current trends seem to indicate that using the mini as a local processor in a network is the direction many libraries will be going. It is as much good luck as good management that we have a system that anticipates this trend. Having it, we intend to exploit our good fortune.

DAVID P. WAITE

President, Information Dynamics Corporation

Reading, Massachusetts

# The Minicomputer:
# Its Role in a Nationwide Bibliographic
# and Information Network

In January 1974, Information Dynamics Corporation introduced to the library community a nationwide on-line bibliographic and information network called BIBNET. Installations have begun and operations are expected to go into full swing in the summer of 1974. Hardware and software systems being installed at user locations, as well as data entry points, employ minicomputers (see figure 1). This paper will describe the several applications of minicomputers in this large-scale computing network.

When BIBNET was first conceived, the decision was made to use minicomputers in order to meet the multipurpose design objectives of a far-reaching nationwide library and information support service. The ultimate objective was not simply the development of a new on-line cataloging system, but the design of a complete service system that would be able to meet successfully future developments in the library community. The network is being established to provide libraries with on-line access to the national data base of machine-readable cataloging records, to provide access to information service modules and for data processing where machine-readable records are available to carry out a number of technical processing operations that in the past have been performed by manual means. Before describing the several system design requirements, it is important to review the basic supporting role and service objectives of the overall bibliographic and information network program.

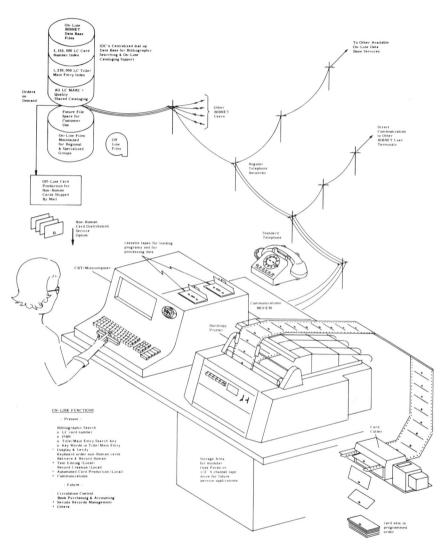

**This diagram depicts the capabilities of each BIBNET user's terminal regardless of location on North American continent. Each CRT/mini-computer terminal has on-line capabilities as shown without need for telephone connections while performing on-line functions identified as (local).**

## Fig. 1. BIBNET Network System

## Background

The purposes to be served by BIBNET are best understood by first noting the communication needs and transactional activities of libraries working together in groups to share in the use of library materials and information resources. Rosenthal recently identified the basic needs of resource sharing as including: (1) a bibliographic access system, (2) a system for delivery of physical material, and (3) an understanding or arrangement for participating libraries to share in the development of and use of their collections of resource materials.[1] Functionally, these three elements are interdependent. Sharing in collection development, for instance, requires knowing who has what on an individual item basis, suggesting the need to have holdings codes information available in the bibliographic access system.

Prior to BIBNET, no nationwide service existed to provide libraries on-line means to access the national bibliographic data base or to communicate with each other via telecommunications. As a result, most library groups desiring to share their resources have had to first devote their energies to building a local or regional system for providing bibliographic access. As a consequence, individual, uncoordinated system development efforts have been threatening the library community with problems of bibliographic confusion.[2] The situation might be paralleled with the early development days of railway systems and telephone companies before their adoption of national standards. BIBNET is a nationwide bibliographic and information access system for the use of all libraries that have access to standard telephone equipment and a BIBNET terminal. Each user library can search the national data base of machine-readable cataloging records, conduct bibliographic transactions with other libraries, and access many on-line information services available from other sources.

## Network Design Objectives

The design of BIBNET responds to the following needs:

1.  The assembly of a much more comprehensive data base of machine-readable LC cataloging records than is now available—retrospective as well as current. Shared cataloging of non-LC records must be included without confusing these with LC cataloging done under the centralized control of name and subject authorities.

2.  A strict adherence to national standards for MARC cataloging records, whether produced at LC or elsewhere, in order to assure compatibility

with bibliographic data processing systems produced by others that follow these standards.

3. Multiple-access indexes that provide more powerful on-line methods for searching the national data base. For example, key-word-in-title, International Standard Book Number as well as LC card number, LC classification number, and series note, plus several others of use to staff and library users.

4. On-line display of holdings codes for libraries participating in groups that may share library materials on one or more levels—first locally, then statewide or regionally, and finally, nationally and internationally. As a minimum, holdings codes should extend to include all holdings reported and published in the National Union Catalog.

5. A cataloging service module that (a) allows the user library to review and revise, when necessary, those records retrieved from the central data base, and (b) provides for the local creation and processing of original cataloging records.

6. Hardcopy equipment options that enable the immediate output printing of data and information search results, interlibrary loan communications, cataloging proof copy, and finished catalog card sets.

7. Automated subsystems for book processing with spine labels and book pockets, the preparation of purchase orders, serials records management, circulation control and other modules.

8. Telecommunications facilities to handle transactions involving bibliographic data and information transmission between libraries.

9. On-line access to information services offered by other suppliers, including those for reference work, such as ERIC, INFORM, National Technical Information Service, New York Times Index, etc.

10. A means for subject searching the national data base.

11. A program for producing frequently updated catalogs by COM or other means that will allow the closing out of large card catalogs when the day comes to switch over from this costly method of catalog maintenance.[3]

Use of the minicomputer accounts for BIBNET's ability to meet objectives 1, 2, 5, 6, 7, 8 and 9. BIBNET service features that respond to the other network design objectives—3, 4, 10 and 11—are also supported by a centralized data base management system and a microfiche production facility not described in this paper.

## Dispersed Computing Facilities

Use of dispersed computing, i.e., a central computer connected to minicomputers installed at user locations, gives the BIBNET network several advantages over the centralized computer approach. Communications costs are reduced and overall system reliability is greatly increased. Work flow is under more direct control of the library staff, and a much larger group of libraries can be served without overloading the central data base management system.

Not all BIBNET users need minicomputers. Many of the smaller libraries will use low-cost communications terminals for on-line searching of information and cataloging data to verify titles and to get the display of holdings codes. Orders can then be keyed in for supporting services like the mailing out of interlibrary loan requests, catalog cards, and book processing kits.

## Minicomputer Equipment and Software

The choice of minicomputers capable of meeting BIBNET applications needs is considerable. As a practical matter, however, we have begun with one general purpose unit, the Datapoint 2200, and developed integrated software program packages to handle most of the initial application needs in the system.

A diagram describing Datapoint 2200 is shown in figure 2. We have found this computer, with its 16K bytes of high-speed memory, integral keyboard, CRT, and plug-in magnetic tape cassettes for program and data handling, to be an ideal general purpose unit for library and information service applications. In instances where a hardcopy printer is needed, the General Electric Terminet is used in conjunction with the Datapoint.

BIBNET software for the minicomputer has all been written in assembly language to achieve the highest possible data processing efficiencies. All programs written to perform interactively with the keyboard operator appear to be on-line whether the minicomputer is functioning while communicating with the central data base management system or while functioning on its own as a stand-alone unit.

## Application to Objectives 1 and 2: Assembly of the National Data Base to National Standards

The BIBNET data base about to be loaded on-line contains all available LC records—a MARC data base of approximately 450,000 full cataloging

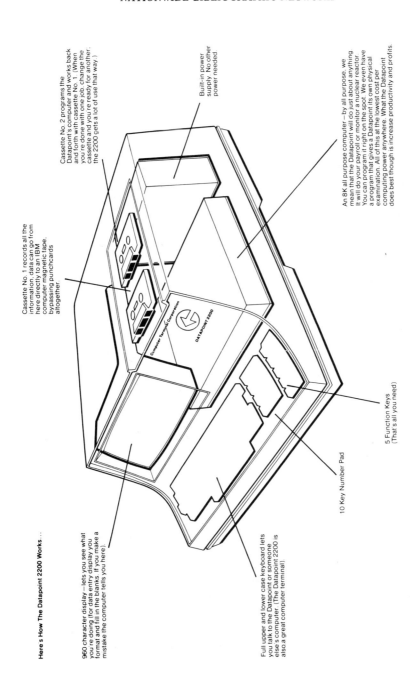

**Here's How The Datapoint 2200 Works...**

**960 character display** — lets you see what you're doing (for data entry display you format and fill in the blanks. If you make a mistake the computer tells you here).

Cassette No. 1 records all the information, data can go from here directly to an IBM computer magnetic tape, bypassing punchcards altogether.

Cassette No. 2 programs the Datapoint's computer and works back and forth with cassette No. 1. (When you're done with one job, change the cassette and you're ready for another, the 2200 gets a lot of use that way.)

Built-in power supply. No other power needed.

An 8K all purpose computer — by all purpose, we mean that the Datapoint will do just about anything. It will do your payroll or monitor a nuclear reactor. You can program it right on the spot. We even have a program that gives a Datapoint its own physical examination. All of this at the lowest cost per computing power anywhere. What the Datapoint does best though is increase productivity and profits

Full upper and lower case keyboard lets you talk to the Datapoint or someone else's computer. (The Datapoint 2200 is also a great computer terminal).

10 Key Number Pad

5 Function Keys
(That's all you need)

**Fig. 2. Datapoint 2200 Layout**

records that meet national standards. In addition, index files containing the title, main entry, and/or LC card number for all 3,550,000 items (including all languages) cataloged by LC since 1953 will be on-line. Holdings codes will appear in the index files and can be assigned to any LC item cataloged in the past 22 years. When a successful search in the index files shows that LC has cataloged the item, but no MARC record currently exists, a command at the keyboard instructs Information Dynamics Corporation to retrieve the LC record, tag it, key it and enter it into the data base. Our target for turnaround time on this, from the time of command to on-line availability, is 96 hours. Subsequent users searching for the same record will have immediate on-line access. In this data base building application, the minicomputer is used first for data entry; second for proof print-out; and third for text editing.

## DATA ENTRY

The specific requirements for data entry are established by national standards for the MARC II communications format for cataloging records. Since BIBNET adheres to these standards without compromise, it was necessary to develop a highly efficient data entry system to keep conversion costs down.

The basic design strategy for BIBNET's MARC II data entry system eliminates all manual table look-up and code memorizing by the keyboard operator. The process of creating a new record begins with a worksheet on which the cataloger enters all textual data as well as both fixed and variable MARC tags.

The worksheet, shown in figure 3, is designed to work conveniently with data entry procedures at the keyboard. With one or two keystrokes, the operator keys in mnemonic tags in the blank spaces shown in the display on the cathode ray tube of the minicomputer. The CRT display for the fixed tags is shown in figure 4. The display for variable tags is shown in figure 5.

After making tag entries, the operator proceeds to key in the full text of the catalog record. Nearly all routine steps are under control of the minicomputer program, e.g., indentation, automatic continuation card set-up, heading generation from tracings, etc. Productivity of the cataloging data entry operation averages eight records per hour, including time for proof printing and corrections. Each cassette has the capacity to hold approximately 200 MARC records. The @ sign appearing in the example shown in figure 6 is used as a single delimiter code for all subfields in the MARC II format structure. An @ sign is always keyed in at the end of each subfield whether or not an entry exists for that subfield. Any subfield in a MARC II record can be identified by its sequential location, thus the data entry operator need not

**BIBNET**

INFORMATION DYNAMICS CORPORATION
80 Main Street, Reading, Massachusetts 01867

CATALOGING WORKSHEET -- Original & Modified Records

Control No:

Date Code __/          Date 1 __/__/__          Date 2 __/__/__

Country __/__/__   Illus __/__/__/__      Level __/      Repro __/      Form __/__/__

Cat Src __/   Code Src __/   Govt Pub __/   Conf __/   Fest __/   Index __/

"by" Main Entry __/   Fiction __/   Biography __/      Lang 1 __/__/__/__

Lang 2 __/__/__/__      Lang 3,4, etc.                              D : S
                                                                     i : u
                                            L.C.                     f : p
Call # Auth. __/__/__/__   Subj. Hdg. Auth. __/__/__/__   Card #_____

| | | |
|---|---|---|
| ME __/ | Main Entry | |
| UTI __/ | Uniform Title | |
| TIL __/ | Title | |
| EDN __/ | Edition | |
| IMP __/ | Imprint | |
| COL __/ | Collation | |
| SE 1 __/__ <br> 2 __/__ <br> 3 __/__ <br> PRI __/__ | Series Statement | Price |
| NO <br> 1. __/ 2. __/ <br> 3. __/ 4. __/ <br> 5. __/ 6. __/ <br> 7. __/ | Note(s) | |
| SU <br> 1. __/__ 2. __/__ <br> 3. __/__ 4. __/__ <br> 5. __/__ 6. __/__ <br> 7. __/__ | Subjects | |
| AE <br> 1. __/__/__ 2. __/__/__ <br> 3. __/__/__ 4. __/__/__ <br> 5. __/__/__ 6. __/__/__ <br> 7. __/__/__ | Added Entries | |

LC CAL __/   DDC CAL __/   LOCAL CAL __/   ISBN __/   NBN __/

OAN __/   GAC __/   (Update Records): LME __/__   LUTI __/   LTIL __/

**Fig. 3. Cataloger's Worksheet for MARC Record Input to BIBNET**

| L C Call # | | Dewey Call # | | | |
|---|---|---|---|---|---|

| Class No. (a) | Book No. or Cutter No. (b) | Added Copy Description (c) | Copy (d) | Location (e) | Accession No. (f) |
|---|---|---|---|---|---|
| | | | | | |

| | ISBN (a) | Binding / Copy ID (b) | Price (c) |
|---|---|---|---|
| **BIBNET**® INFORMATION DYNAMICS CORPORATION 80 Main Street, Reading, Massachusetts 01867  CATALOGING WORKSHEET | | | |

| NBN | OAN | GAC |
|---|---|---|

**Update Records Only**

| Local Main Entry | |
|---|---|
| Local Uniform Title | |
| Local Title | |

Prepared by: _____  Date: _____

Keyed by: _____  Date: _____

Proofread by: _____  Date: _____

Cassette # _____

9-track tape # _____

**Fig. 3. (continued)**

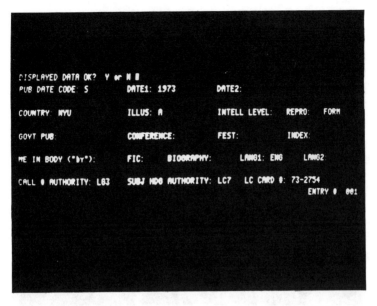

**Fig. 4. BIBNET Terminal Display: Fixed Tags for MARC Input**

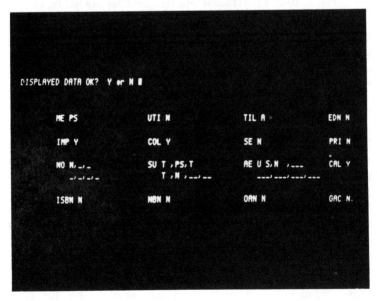

**Fig. 5. BIBNET Terminal Display: Variable Tags for MARC Input**

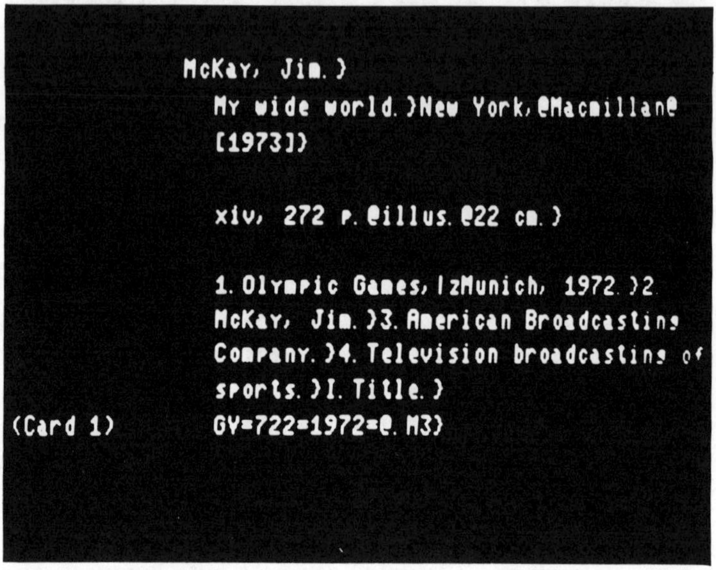

McKay, Jim. )
My wide world. )New York, @Macmillan@
[1973])

xiv, 272 p. @illus. @22 cm. )

1. Olympic Games, l zMunich, 1972. )2.
McKay, Jim. )3. American Broadcasting
Company. )4. Television broadcasting of
sports. )I. Title. )
(Card 1)          GV=722=1972=@. M3)

**Fig. 6. BIBNET Terminal Display: Text for MARC Input**

assign unique codes to these subfield delimiters. A post-data entry processing routine performed automatically by the minicomputer accomplishes the generation of these codes when formatting the fully tagged MARC II record.

## PROOF COPY

After initial data entry is completed, records can be printed out for proofing under the control of the minicomputer proof-print program that drives an impact printer. The minicomputer is equipped with two cassette tape decks, shown in figure 7, that enable the operator to change computer programs and data as desired in moving from one job to the next. The printer proof-prints an exploded MARC record, shown in figure 8. After proofreading and annotation by catalogers for corrections, the proof copy is then returned to the keyboard operator for text editing.

## TEXT EDITING

When editing cataloging recorded on cassette tape, the cassette is inserted in tape deck position 1. The text editing program is then read into

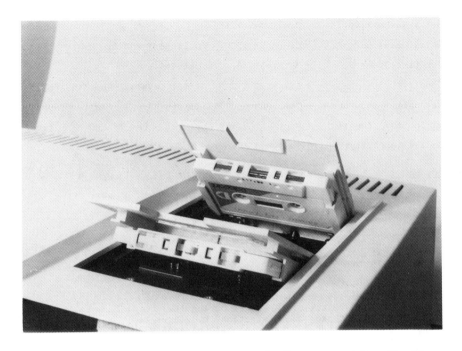

**Fig. 7. Datapoint 2200 with Cassette Tapes for Programs and Data Handling**

the minicomputer's internal memory, and a blank tape is mounted in tape deck position 2. The text editing routines used are comprehensive, allowing for insertion of characters and words with automatic rewrite of the line, deletions, line spacing and other features necessary to fully text edit in accordance with annotations on the proof copy. Each record is corrected while in the computer's high-speed memory, before being released and re-corded on the cassette in position 2. Records are copied without change from the original-entry cassette to the corrected-copy cassette if no editing is required. The finished result is a cassette of corrected records in proper sequence and format ready for subsequent processing and use. These cassette records can be used immediately or set aside and used later with subsequent processing routines. For assembly of the centralized BIBNET data base, MARC II records are first read onto standard half-inch nine-track tape using the tape drive hardware module shown in figure 9 to produce MARC tapes with form and content just like those received from LC.

Data recorded on the half-inch nine-track tape is forwarded to BIBNET Data Central to be loaded, along with surrogate indexes, into the master

```
Entry Number: 001          Control No: 1

Entry Date: 05/15/74       Library: IDC      Operator: BJC

Pub Date Code: S           Date1: 1973       Date2:

Country: MSU               Illus:            Intel Level:   Repro:    Form:

Cat Src:   Code Src:       Govt Pub:         Conf:          Fest:    Index: 1

ME in Body ('by'): 1       Fic:    Biography:      Lang1: ENG       Lang2:

Call # Authority: HL3      Subj Hdg Authy: HL1   LC Card #: 73-00000


ME: PS                     UTI: N           TIL: A         EDN: N

IMP: Y                     COL: Y           SE: N , ,      PRI: Y

NO: G,B,N , , , ,          SU: T ,T ,T ,N , , ,

                           AE: U S,N , , , , ,            CAL: Y

DDC CAL: N                 LOC.CAL: Y

ISBN: Y                    NBN: N           OAN: N         GAC: N
```

```
       Harvey James c:d1925-)
          Black civil rights during the
       Johnson administration@[by] James C.
       Harvey.)Jackson [Miss.]@University and
       college press of Mississippi@[c1973])

       xiv, 245 p.@tables.@21 1/2 cm.)
       $4.95)

       "...a sequel to the earlier volume,
       Civil rights during the Kennedy admin-
       istration.")


          Bibliography: p. 227_239.)              (Card 2)

          1.Civil rights:z--United States)
          2.Negroes:z--United States)3.Politics
          and government:z--United States:y
          __1963-)I.Title)
    CAL:      US=962.4=HAR)
    LOC.CAL: AB=123=@XY:d01@AN:d02@wo:d03@AL)
    ISBN:    0-87805-02103)
```

**Fig. 8. Proof Printout for Review and Annotation**

on-line files and made available to on-line users of the bibliographic network. In BIBNET, the keying of all records added to the national data base is a centrally performed, highly controlled operation. The central BIBNET file management system will accept original cataloging of users entered directly from remote terminals, but these records are tagged so as not to be confused

**Fig. 9. Datapoint Tape Drive Records MARC II Records**

with national data base records that have been given careful quality control to assure their full compliance with MARC II standards.

## Application to Objectives 3, 4 and 5: Bibliographic Search, Record Retrieval and Library Use

Interactive searching of BIBNET's centralized bibliographic files requires only a communications terminal. However, for the medium and larger libraries using BIBNET, a minicomputer with CRT display, keyboard, and accompanying printer is installed to provide general purpose computer power needed for printing finished catalog cards on site, for proof-printing and text editing of retrieved records. Future service modules for book fund accounting, circulation control, serials records management, and others will require use of the minicomputer. The economies of these modules, when available, will make use of the minicomputer attractive to some of the smaller libraries as well.

## ON-LINE SEARCHING

For use in on-line searching, the minicomputer has been programmed to emulate a CRT communications terminal. Its properties as a minicomputer are not fully utilized in this application, but greater use will be made in the near future when a semiautomatic re-search feature is added to the BIBNET service. When this feature is available, the operator will load a cassette containing a cumulation of previous search statements of items not yet cataloged. With a single key stroke, each can be released to initiate re-searches for materials waiting on the holding-shelf for cataloging copy.

Most of the program software responsible for the BIBNET system's exceptionally powerful on-line search features reside in the centralized data management system. Searching can be done by LC card number, ISBN, title, key-words-in-title, Ruecking algorithm, main entry, series note, LC call number, publication date, IDC's identification number, data file update, or combinations of the above.

## VERIFYING

Following a search of the data base using these index terms individually or in combination, the number-count of file postings or "hits" matching the search statement is displayed. Search procedures provide the means for rapidly narrowing down to the items desired. Next, selected data elements from the full cataloging record are displayed, including title, main entry, imprint, classification number, call number, ISBN, publication date and status symbol. This display enables the operator to verify that the records resulting from the search are the desired records and to observe holdings codes. The multiple access search features combined with Boolean search logic generally allows the search to be quickly narrowed down to one posting. In the event that multiple postings are to be examined by the searcher (e.g., before making the decision to retrieve) and for those searchers who simply want to examine holdings codes, the verifying mode can be expanded to display this information. It allows examination of the major data elements of any number of records prior to giving a full catalog record retrieval command.

## RETRIEVING

After verifying each available record, the keyboard operator commands the system to transmit the full MARC record to the minicomputer terminal where it is recorded on a cassette tape. The cycle of search, verify, and retrieve is then repeated for the next title. When searching by unique index terms such as LC card number or ISBN, the search, verify and retrieve cycle takes less than 40 seconds. Approximately 100 records per hour can be searched and retrieved from the central data base. During these operations, the minicomputer is connected by telephone through the communications modem with the centralized BIBNET data base management system.

After all desired records are retrieved in this manner and recorded on the minicomputer cassette tape, the telephone connection to BIBNET data central can be terminated and all subsequent operations performed using the hardware and software of the minicomputer system installed in the library as a free-standing facility.

## PROOF PRINTOUT

The same minicomputer program for proof printout described above for the data base assembly application is provided to user libraries. This is used in reviewing and revising records retrieved prior to the addition of these records to library catalog files. Proof printout and review prior to use of the record for production of catalog cards or other entries into the library's bibliographic apparatus is important to the integrity of the catalogs in most large libraries. The cataloging problem answered by this feature is best described by Ohmes and Jones in their article on "The Other Half of Cataloging."[5] With BIBNET, records retrieved from the national data base can be examined for correctness and compared for compatibility with subject and name authorities used locally. Catalogers working with "proof" printout enjoy full mobility of the record and have the means for annotating desired changes. This way, hard copy instructions are provided to the keyboard operator for use in revising retrieved machine-readable records before entering into the shelflist file or making catalog cards.

## EDITING

Employing the same editing software described above, the operator at the user library location can make changes according to annotations made by the cataloging staff. Working from the annotated proof copy, the operator calls up the desired record by keying in its unique entry number. This allows the sequential review and correction of fixed and variable tags followed by full text in a manner identical to that described earlier for the centralized data base assembly application.

The minicomputer program automatically handles all routine features of formatting. However, these can be modified to suit individual library requirements, e.g., accommodating unique call number notations and any desired rules for indentations and/or placement of data elements. Headings can appear in upper and lower case with initial caps only or be displayed as all caps. Any data elements not desired on finished cards, such as LC card number, or unused classification numbers, can be automatically suppressed. If the cataloging record flows over into continuation cards, these are automatically generated to match the requirements of the printer used for production of fully headed sets of cards.

## ORIGINAL CATALOGING DATA ENTRY

The same software data entry package used to assemble the central data base in MARC II format is supplied to library users. If the library's original cataloging data entry is to be captured in machine-readable form for further use, it is suggested that the procedures for full tagging and complete MARC record entry be followed. If the user library desires not to follow this practice, the fixed and variable tag displays can be skipped over and just the text composed for the automatic production of cards. The same proof printout programs, full text editing and card printing programs can be used to handle original cataloging card production in the same manner as those retrieved from the centralized data base.

## Application to Objectives 6 and 7:
## Output Printing and Additional Service Modules

### OUTPUT PRINTING

Use of the BIBNET network provides the library with a machine-readable record that has been transmitted to its minicomputer terminal immediately after the result of a successful search (exceptions during data base assembly are noted earlier). All steps of review and edit are then under the direct control of the library staff. Adding high quality impact printing capability to the facilities installed at the minicomputer location makes processing results immediately available. It also provides the advantage of having close quality control over library work flow right through to the point of finished product. When an error is made, it is readily detected and corrective action can be taken without difficulty right on the spot.

The Datapoint 2200 can drive a variety of impact printers. The printer chosen for use in most BIBNET installations is the General Electric Terminet unit—a proven device backed up by worldwide field service. A major platen modification was necessary to handle the feeding of card stock properly (see figure 10). Both low-speed and high-speed units are available running at speeds of 30 or 120 characters per second. The basic unit has surprisingly few moving parts. It uses a belt printer mechanism potentially capable of being modified to meet the ALA character-set requirements. The paper feed mechanism is tractor type to accurately feed card stock for the printing of catalog cards or multipart forms for other applications.

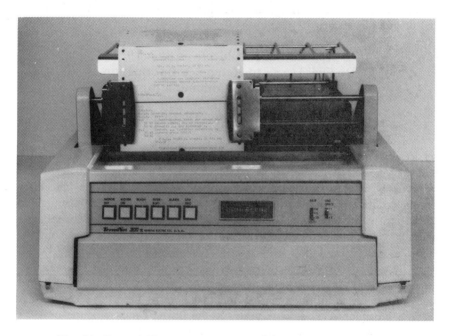

**Fig. 10. General Electric Terminet Modified to Feed Card Stock**

### ADDITIONAL SERVICE MODULES

Many libraries have already invested in automation of their technical processing operations. These include acquisition support and accounting systems, serials records management systems, circulation control and others. The BIBNET service was designed to be highly flexible in order to work with a variety of existing bibliographic data processing systems. Any system that operates with MARC II input tapes can use the BIBNET on-line service to access the national data base for the immediate electronic delivery of compatible machine-readable cataloging records.

The BIBNET minicomputer terminal, with its many features, has the compute power to perform data processing tasks for acquisitions and accounting systems, serials records management, circulation control and other needs. Support module subsystems are being prepared for future release as part of the BIBNET program. These modules will work in close conjunction with the initial on-line cataloging support module described in this paper. Additional minicomputer peripheral equipment will be used with these service modules, including tape drives and disk storage units for handling both batch and on-line processing.

## Application to Objectives 8 and 9:
## On-line Access to Reference Information
## and Interlibrary Communications

### ACCESS TO REFERENCE INFORMATION

Libraries must provide access to the variety of on-line information services now beginning to come into the market. Most of these provide for bibliographic search in support of reference work. Capturing the bibliographic citations of interest with the minicomputer makes possible the immediate printing and distribution of search results to the research user. Semiautomatic processing of these citations for interlibrary loan, photocopy service requests and the preparation of purchase orders for report reprints are next obvious steps.

By policy, BIBNET encourages its users to use the BIBNET terminal to access the many data bases available. We take the position that our information services are in an open market and that libraries need full access to that market. Programmable compute power in the BIBNET minicomputer provides the technical means for adapting the terminal to meet different on-line data service system requirements like baud rate, half- or full-duplex, automatic dial-up, as well as code structures, message formats and other details of the communications interface.

The BIBNET terminal gives the user library flexibility in accessing just about any on-line service that is made available through the standard dial-up telephone network. In this way, we have eliminated the need for the library to make multiple equipment investments for a variety of data services being offered by different suppliers.

### INTERLIBRARY COMMUNICATIONS

In 1972, the Association of Research Libraries initiated a feasibility study under the acronym SILC—System for Interlibrary Loan Communications. This study starts with the premise that interlibrary loan transactions will greatly increase in the near future. It suggests that the efficiency of handling these transactions can be greatly improved through the use of a computer-to-computer communications network.[6] The designers of BIBNET believe this is a logical expectation. Widespread trends to automate the bibliographic apparatus of libraries, coupled with increased pressures to share resource materials, point the way for this future development.

Besides having the compute power to handle future automated interlibrary loan terminal communications needs, the minicomputer employed by BIBNET users has a number of features that are currently useful for general communications between libraries. Consider, for instance, even without the future discipline of a mechanized interlibrary loan system as the proposed SILC, how the BIBNET terminal can be applied to present practices used in interlibrary loan. Dial-up and keyboard action is as convenient as a teletype. The programs available allow the minicomputer terminal to simulate a teletype unit. It can be used to communicate with libraries that use standard teletypes interconnected by the standard telephone network. The cassette tape feature permits off-line composition of intricate or long messages. Likewise, the cassette tape record feature permits the receiving and recording of long messages transmitted at high speed. These features provide the means for high-volume, high-speed information message transmission from one library to another at minimum communication costs. They are already built into the BIBNET minicomputer terminal.

The application of these capabilities to future developments in interlibrary loan practices will be easy to achieve. Use of the impact printer at the terminal will further add to the flexibility of transmitting bibliographic data and reference information assuring immediate hard copy access for both staff and library users.

## Network Service Objectives 10 and 11:
## Subject Searching and COM Catalogs

### SUBJECT SEARCHING

Characteristics of the minicomputer, other than its use as an on-line terminal, appear to offer no unique advantages at this time in searching the national data base by subject. Indirectly, however, it plays a role supporting subject searching when employed in the assembly of the centralized BIBNET data base. When searches of transliterated titles in the BIBNET index files result in a request for cataloging data, the service meets these requests by furnishing graphic copy sent through the mails. There is no intent at this time to handle character-sets beyond ALA standards in the computer-based network. There will, however, be a partial MARC record created for each non-Roman LC-cataloged item with properly tagged main entry, transliterated title, subject headings (in English), and all other data elements that can be captured by the standard character-set. One of these elements is a microfiche file address where the full graphic LC card image can be found.

At a future time, if market demand is sufficient, searching of the centralized data base by subject headings may be offered. In the interim, the key-word-in-title search feature of BIBNET is an effective way to conduct a rudimentary subject search. It provides no specificity other than that provided by authors and publishers on their choice of words for titles, but one can locate useful material on practically any subject. Since the national data base of cataloging records is so vast, materials on even the most obscure subject can be readily found by combining key-word-in-title with a cut-off date of publication, the latter to limit the number of hits. The centralized BIBNET data base can be searched by classification number as well, giving another approach to subject searching.

## COM-PRODUCED CATALOGS

One BIBNET user institution with multiple campuses is preparing to have us supply COM-produced catalogs by subject, title and author. This service will soon be offered to other BIBNET users requiring only that they capture their bibliographic data in machine readable-form meeting MARC standards.

COM is seen as one method for accomplishing a close-out of the conventional card catalog by institutions which have that desire. Capture of all subject headings in English, plus the transliterated titles and main entries described above, will make it possible to construct COM-produced catalogs containing indicia for all records including non-Roman alphabet items.

Besides offering economies in reduced catalog maintenance costs for large institutions, the COM-produced catalogs offer a means for meeting projected needs for the "open campus" or "university without walls."[7] We believe COM-produced catalogs will become a logical supplement to on-line bibliographic systems in meeting the wide spectrum of future user services.

Used in conjunction with the large-scale network design approach of dispersed computing, the minicomputer has made it possible to meet the several challenging applications requirements outlined for the BIBNET nationwide bibliographic and information service network.

The resulting network will (1) accommodate national, regional, and local bibliographic needs for technical processing and information resource sharing;

(2) enable the interconnection of all types of libraries (both private and public) as well as data and information analysis centers in order to facilitate the exchange of bibliographic data, information and interlibrary loan related transaction messages; (3) enable users connected to one node to have access to any other node; (4) have no geographic limits within North America; and (5) adhere strictly to the MARC II bibliographic standards for cataloging and use standard telephone circuits in conjunction with the international Tymshare computer communications network. Thanks to the flexibility, compute power, and relatively low cost of the minicomputer, BIBNET is prepared to meet current library service needs economically with built-in capacity for substantial growth and assurances against obsolescence as future needs for library and information services develop.

## REFERENCES

1. Rosenthal, Joseph. Paper presented at ALA Information Sciences and Automation Division Institute (Alternatives of Bibliographic Networking), Feb. 28-March 1, 1974, New Orleans, La.

2. *A Proposal for "A New National Program of Library and Information Service."* Washington, D.C., National Commission on Libraries and Information Science, Oct. 1973.

3. Fussler, Herman H. *Research Libraries and Technology.* Chicago, University of Chicago Press, 1973.

4. Ruecking, Frederick H., Jr. "Bibliographic Retrieval from Bibliographic Input; The Hypothesis and Construction of a Test," *Journal of Library Automation*, 1:227-38, Dec. 1968.

5. Ohmes, Frances, and Jones, J. F. "The Other Half of Cataloging," *Library Resources & Technical Services*, 17:320-29, Summer 1973.

6. Becker, Joseph. "Library Networks: The Beacon Lights." *In* F. Wilfrid Lancaster, ed. *Proceedings of the 1973 Clinic on Library Applications of Data Processing: Networking and Other Forms of Cooperation.* Urbana-Champaign, University of Illinois Graduate School of Library Science, 1973, pp. 171-79.

7. Waite, David P. *Library Networks—Book 1.* Reading, Mass., Information Dynamics Corp., 1972.

AUDREY N. GROSCH
Bio-Medical Library Mini-Computer Project
University of Minnesota
Minneapolis, Minnesota

# Minicomputer—Characteristics, Economics and Selection for an Integrated Library Management System

## Misconceptions about Minicomputers

When the term "minicomputer" initially was coined it denoted a physically small, low-cost computer using available technology and designed to perform a specific function. Usage of these devices was limited mainly to the laboratory, certain process-dependent industrial tasks, and special-purpose computational problems. Today, the minicomputer is no longer limited to such systems. However, not all computing specialists, library systems analysts, and librarians realize that the situation is rapidly changing and will continue to do so. Sometimes the feelings one experiences when discussing minicomputers, particularly as independent processors, may be conveyed by the following verse:

> Automation
> Is Vexation,
> Quarternions are bad;
> Analysis Situs
> Is only detritus
> I wonder: Have I been had?[1]

The misconceptions which were based on the qualities of minicomputers until the last few years were:

1. slow instruction execution time and cycle time,
2. small memory with lack of expansion,
3. lack of peripheral equipment,

4. lack of peripheral device interfaces,
5. low reliability and unsatisfactory maintenance services,
6. poor programming instruction sets,
7. lack of vendor-supplied software,
8. greater programming difficulty,
9. lack of character addressability,
10. lack of hardware multiply and divide, and
11. image as front-end processors requiring large host computers for file updating and output processing.

This paper seeks to dispel these misconceptions in the broad sense, although one can see that individual minicomputers have specific strengths and weaknesses dependent upon the end application use. The minicomputers considered here are machines available currently and developed in the last two to three years.

## Minicomputer Systems

A minicomputer system is normally composed of a processor, memory, and selected peripheral devices for input, storage and output of data. In other words, the mini may have much the same peripheral equipment as any other computer system. Minicomputers have always employed the technology available at their time of development just as have any other central processors. The technical differences between mini and nonmini systems are that minicomputers usually have shorter word lengths, fewer machine programming instructions, and most of their peripheral devices are designed for use with minicomputers—matched to their speed needs and their prices. A single nontechnical difference is that the price of the minicomputer system will be from 10 percent to 30 percent of that of systems judged in the small- to large-scale hardware classes. Let us look in greater detail at the system components.

### PROCESSORS

With nearly fifty manufacturers of processors in the United States, there are many to be considered. In choosing the processor and other parts of the system one must define the tasks required to service the envisioned application needs. There are two main minicomputer architectural types to consider— single bus and multiple bus, with the latter the most common. Processors such as Hewlett Packard, Data General's Nova line, and Varian use the multiple bus structure shown in figure 1. The single bus concept is used by DEC in their PDP 11 family. The Bio-Medical Mini-Computer System at the University of Minnesota shown in figure 2 illustrates this architecture.

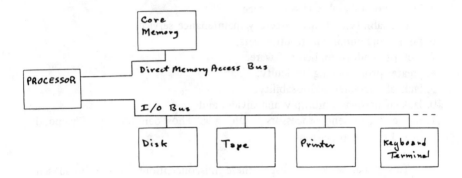

**Fig. 1. Multiple Bus Minicomputer System**

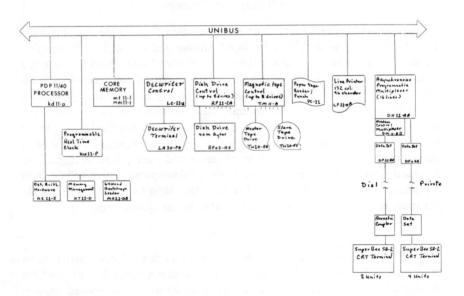

**Fig. 2. Univerity of Minnesota Bio-Medical Library PDP 11/40 Computer System**

The single bus structure gives the user greater flexibility to add or change devices attached to the bus, even mixing memories of differing speeds. Further, the I/O devices may communicate directly with memory without processor involvement. The disadvantage in the single bus structure is its greater design complexity since it must accommodate both high- and low-density bit transmission. Multiple bus systems are simple to design and also provide direct memory access, but usually at extra cost, and usually then require a separate channel for each device.

Word lengths of miniprocessors vary from 8 to 32 bits, with 16 bits the most common in current machines, and 24- and 32-bit machines just now coming into the market place at prices very competitive to some 16-bit machines. For library use a multiple of 8 bits is most desirable. The advantage of a larger word size is that more memory may be directly addressed as well as increasing the transfer rate of data. Moreover, the larger word size machines have larger instruction sets. But word length alone cannot determine processor choice; the appropriate instruction set must also be available.

Other processor features such as number of registers, addressing techniques, power fail/automatic restart, real-time clock, and additional processor options must be considered since typically miniprocessors have definite strengths and weaknesses when considered for use in a specific application area.

Generally, the processors currently available range from 330 nanoseconds to 1.2 microseconds per word memory cycle time with memory size of 8K-124K words permitted. They will also have from 1 to 5 accumulators, 0 to 24 index registers (or some comparable range of general purpose registers), and interrupt levels ranging from 2 to a variable number. The register arrangement, the number of interrupt levels, and the specific addressing modes permitted is an indicator of programming flexibility and ease.

## MEMORY

Minicomputer memories are usually magnetic core construction, but semiconductor memories also are available on some processors. The MOS (metal-oxide semiconductor) and bipolar memories are very fast—from 300-450 nanoseconds but, of course, currently at greater cost than core memories in the 600-900 nanosecond range. The memory speed and size is available to support any library data processing task in an on-line integrated data management system. Even without increasing memory speed, which can many times be added from another manufacturer later, today's minisystems offer more throughput than past and some presently used conventional systems. Current memory technology is bringing memory cost down rapidly so that memory cost for an application is not restrictive. Most processors can accommodate up to 64K bytes equivalent memory and a reasonable number beyond this. Memory protection, if offered, is normally an extra cost option associated with the larger memory configurations.

### PERIPHERAL EQUIPMENT

Today, it is possible to interface virtually any current peripheral device to a minicomputer. This interface is independent of the brand of processor, but obviously the larger manufacturer's machines will tend to have ready-made interfaces for larger numbers of peripheral devices. The leading mini manufacturers offer many peripheral devices. More than 100 manufacturers are currently in the mini peripheral equipment marketplace. If ready-made interfaces are not available there are custom system houses which will interface virtually any device to any processor. One can choose peripherals from among the following categories:

1. Fixed head disks for program swapping use with capacities to 250,000 bytes.
2. Floppy disks, as a cheaper, usually slower alternative to the above with similar capacities.
3. Moving head disks with capacities from 1.2K bytes to 86K bytes per cartridge or pack, with up to 8 drives controllable per controller, at costs from $9,000 to $300 per million bytes or approximately $7.50 to $.25 per MARC catalog entry.
4. Tape drives, industry compatible or units such as dual density DEC tape, usually with 45 ips speed—slow but adequate.
5. Impact and nonimpact printers which range from $4,000 to $20,000 and give slow to medium print speeds. Many have upper/lower case and some offer character-set extensions such as those with point plotting capability or chain cartridges such as the Data Products Charaband Printer.
6. Cassette tape units for software package and diagnostic support, replacing paper tape units at equivalent prices.
7. Visual and hard copy keyboard terminals with both hard wired and private or dial-access telephone communications arrangements.
8. Special purpose peripherals such as plotters, graphic line drawing displays, digitizers, Rand tablet devices, and a variety of sensors of various types.

There is a slight advantage to minimizing the number of manufacturers involved with the computer system from a maintenance and administrative viewpoint, although this depends upon the geographic area and the size of the system. One can see from this overview that properly chosen minicomputer systems have many hardware features that make them attractive for file- and message-oriented processing.

## INSTRUCTION SET AND SUPPLIED SOFTWARE

When considering the foregoing factors about hardware, one must consider the instruction set of the machine and relate this to the hardware features to determine if the processor will be suited to the application. Library systems require byte and bit manipulation instructions. Some of the more powerful systems have hardware features found on large-scale computers which ease programming and enhance throughput, such as hardware stacks, and extended instruction sets with hardware features to match, such as hardware byte manipulation.

Many, if not most, minicomputers are weak in data test type instructions as they have no Compare instruction, and thus require a complicated sequence of instructions to effect arithmetic comparison. Some machines also do not have direct bit testing capability—a must for library applications. Shift/rotate instructions normally are not of the multiple shift type, i.e., one instruction must be executed for each bit position that the word is to be shifted. Instructions such as Translate also are not found on minicomputers, but such functions can be carried out through use of macros in the programming.

Although various compilers are available for minicomputers, they are not desirable for use in an on-line data management system due to the excessive overhead required. Assemblers, primarily of the two-pass type, and some macro assemblers are the most common programming languages. Macro assemblers such as used with the DEC's PDP 11/40 are quite powerful and well suited to on-line data management system development.

Manufacturer-supplied software usually consists of very minimal operating systems, an assembler, an editor and a linker. The editor enables program code to be altered via keyboard. The linker attaches assembled code to other programs. Operating systems for the most part are single-user systems which support either tape or disk and enable running the assembler, the text editor and the linker. Some other utility functions are usually provided, such as tape-to-disk copying. Some batch operating systems are offered and a few multiuser timesharing systems are available but these provide only single-language support (either BASIC or FORTRAN). Some real time executives also are offered which are usable primarily in an industrial control or analog/digital laboratory data acquisition and monitoring system.

Therefore, the library user will have to use what is provided in a development mode and create his own software, including any operating system functions which are required. There is an advantage to this in that the single dedicated system does not need an operating system of the overhead and complexity featured on typical large systems. Lourey speaks to this point in his discussion of the design of the University of Minnesota Bio-Medical Library Mini-Computer system elsewhere in this volume.

One of the benefits of projects such as the University of Minnesota Bio-Medical Mini-Computer System is to develop data management software amenable to use in many libraries, thereby enabling common software maintenance, lower software costs, and careful testing of system enhancements for use throughout the various libraries. Now let us see how all of the above relates to the on-line library management system.

## On-line Library Management System Needs

Most libraries of significant size either are in the process of deciding to develop new or first systems, are enhancing present systems, or are installing completely reworked systems using different hardware and software. The traditional library applications of ordering, accounting, in-process control, cataloging, serials management, and circulation comprise a complex data base dependent system. Data entered and used in one process may carry over to other processes, with or without change.

Multiple entry point retrieval is required for many functions. Moreover, the size of the data base and the transaction load may be very large. For these reasons, an integrated data base system functions best when hosted on a dedicated computer system. However, because of the inherent cost of large computers, and the fact that library data processing systems are I/O bound, we try to share the computer, ideally with jobs requiring more processor service than I/O service. To do this, however, we must have a complex resource management system, consuming a large portion of machine resources, to oversee such multiple use.

A good way for the library to determine if it should use a shared system or acquire a minicomputer system is to answer the following questions:

1.  Does the proposed shared system have on-line capabilities and sufficient disk storage?
2.  Are those capabilities expandable to fit the library's needs for the next five years or for the expected life of the hardware?
3.  What will be the library's portion of hardware and storage costs for the shared system?

4. Does our application require control over the hardware system configuration to avoid inconvenient or costly program alterations?
5. Is our priority and use high in the computer center?
6. Does the library have its own programming staff or is it able to acquire its own programmer?
7. Is the purchase of a minicomputer system equal to or less than the estimated computer center charges for three years?

These questions will help to isolate the capabilities and costs of the shared system as opposed to the dedicated minicomputer system. If the library is intending to proceed toward a completely on-line system for its data base needs and is sizable enough to acquire its own programming staff, the choice of a dedicated minicomputer system should be made, as the system development costs will be amortized through lower operations costs accompanied by a higher quality system at the user level. Moreover, the library can control the system, enhancing or changing equipment or software as its processing needs change. This will further improve the long-term system economics.

To summarize, there are three points to be considered in coming to a decision on a minicomputer system versus the shared large system: (1) the economics of the system, (2) the performance of the system, and (3) the control over the system.

System economics and performance are discussed in detail by Lourey elsewhere in this volume. Control over the system relates to being able to determine the future of the system as well as assure its current operational status. The library administrator will find both program maintenance and enhancement to be far easier if the programming staff are part of the library rather than having prime responsibility to a data processing center management. An alternate arrangement for control is to use contract services to develop and support a system. However, this really requires that the library have someone with a technical background able to develop the system specifications in considerable detail and then work with the contractor to refine them, code the programs, debug them, test and install the system. With good management, the least costly approach is in-house development of the system. Brudvig discusses this control and library view of the system in detail elsewhere in this volume.

## Choosing a Minicomputer System

After a decision has been made to acquire a dedicated minicomputer system, the specific features of processors and their instruction sets must be evaluated. In addition, decisions on peripheral equipment will have to be made. All of these decisions will be made in light of the applicability of the equipment to perform the tasks required, the ability of the vendor or vendors to keep the equipment operating, and the purchase/maintenance costs of the system.

In order to solicit bids on the equipment and inform the prospective equipment suppliers of its needs, the library should prepare a set of hardware/ system specifications. This document should provide basic system requirements and conditions of procurement. For a full system, with processor and peripheral equipment, the document should contain:

1.  a brief technical description of the proposed system's functions and data base content,
2.  any specific system details known to be required by the application,
3.  processor hardware and instruction set features required or desired,
4.  peripheral equipment devices required,
5.  details of system acquisition if several stages of equipment additions are planned beyond the initial order,
6.  maintenance service provisions desired from the vendor,
7.  software supplied and prices of specific software such as assemblers, editors, operating systems, if not included in hardware costs,
8.  delivery schedules and method of shipment vendor provides, and
9.  evaluation criteria on which the vendor's bid will be judged.

To illustrate some of the above points the University of Minnesota Bio-Medical Library Mini-Computer system vendor document contained the following requirements for the processor:

1.  CPU must be 8-bit byte oriented, with main memory addressable by byte location and preferred word size a multiple of 8 bits,
2.  either explicit character manipulation instructions or some reasonable method of effecting these within the available instruction set,
3.  multilevel indirect addressing and indexing or their functional equivalents are required,
4.  multilevel indexing is desirable but not required,
5.  main memory must be incrementable to at least 64K bytes,
6.  direct memory access required,
7.  real time clock required,
8.  hardware multiply/divide required,
9.  power fail/automatic restart required,

10. memory protection required, and
11. operator console keyboard/printer with 30 cps speed required.

The bidders on this sytem were judged on their:

1. capability to support both hardware and software to be used during development,
2. capability to supply all of the required equipment exclusive of terminals and telecommunications interfaces,
3. delivery schedule,
4. equipment being suitable to character manipulation and library data management system applications, and
5. equipment costs and continued maintenance costs.

To illustrate the outcome of this process let us look at the result of the bidding. We received seven bids on the system. All were very similar in price, except for one, if each vendor had bid identical peripheral equipment according to the specifications. However, vendors did not bid the specified peripherals in most cases. One vendor bid a special purpose minicomputer completely outside the processor specifications. Another vendor bid one minicomputer instead of another one newly added to his equipment family which did fit the specifications quite closely. There are many ways to judge such bids. Several articles have been written which use a formula to show price/performance.[2] However, price/performance alone cannot determine if the system will be well suited to the library problem. The library programming staff must make the final judgment as they have the responsibility to deliver the functioning system and keep it running.

## Vendor Relations

Vendors have different pricing policies for equipment. Most offer educational or governmental discounts up to 10 percent, although some specific equipment which they may procure from other manufacturers may not be discounted. Also, after initial system installation there are additional charges for field installation of system additions. What the initial equipment order should contain should be carefully considered.

Service arrangements also vary among vendors. The safest arrangement is an 8-hour service contract which can be purchased for one year on all or part of the system. On-call maintenance or a combination of on-call with the above is the next most common arrangement. On service contracts there usually is a discount of up to 8 percent for prepayment for the year. Moreover, additional discounts may be available depending upon the number of systems the vendor sells that year or has sold in the past year to the parent institution. These arrangements should be investigated carefully as worthwhile amounts of money can be reallocated to other use.

Another important point is to have the physical space for the system ready when it is delivered. The vendor will be able to help determine the right number and capacity of electric circuits, receptacles, and grounding requirements. Also, be sure the room temperature can be maintained under 75°F in the area of the equipment as tapes and disks, as well as programmers, are subject to temperature and humidity excesses. The processors can withstand rather high operating temperatures, but it is best to provide good ventilation and climate control even to the point of installing a window air conditioning unit.

There will be problems with the first installation. Reconcile yourself to contending with late equipment deliveries and some malfunctions, particularly in disks and their controllers. Keep after the vendor. This is a normal condition in the data processing equipment field, so plan accordingly.

Hopefully, some minicomputer misconceptions have been cleared away by looking into their general characteristics and the decision-making process which may result in their specification for a system. Guidelines for developing that specification as well as suggestions on how to evaluate the resultant vendor proposals should enable librarians to seriously consider the dedicated mini for the library. As an additional aid to those investigating this field a bibliography of current literature is included in this paper.

Earlier, I quoted a verse applicable to the minicomputer's initial entry in libraries. I will close with another applicable verse:

> Geniac, Geniac,
> Digital miracle,
> Giving an answer that's
> Truly empirical,
> Learned men, lost in a
> Drawjopping daze,
> Watch six-year-old Seniors, all
> Grabbing off As![1]

## REFERENCES

1. Windsor, Frederick. *The Space Child's Mother Goose*. New York, Simon and Schuster, 1958.
2. See, for example: Butler, J. L. "Comparative Criteria for Mini-computers," *Instrumentation Technology*, 17:67-82, Oct. 1970.

## ADDITIONAL REFERENCES

DataPro Research Corporation. *All About Mini-Computers*. Moorestown, N.J., 1973.

Gruenberger, Fred, and Babcock, David. "Speaking of Minis," *Datamation*, 19:57-59, July 1973.

————. *Computing with Mini-Computers*. New York, Wiley, 1973.

"In Your Future: Distributed Systems?" *EDP Analyzer*, Vol. 11, Aug. 1973.

Kenney, Donald P. *Mini-computers, Low Cost Computer Power for Management*. New York, AMACOM, 1973.

"The Mini-Computer's Quiet Revolution," *EDP Analyzer*, Vol. 10, Dec. 1972.

Ollivier, Robin T. "A Technique for Selecting Small Computers," *Datamation*, 16:141-45, Jan. 1970.

Schoeffler, James D., and Temple, Ronald H., eds. *Minicomputers: Hardware, Software, and Applications*. New York, IEEE Press, 1972. (Collection of all important articles on minicomputers up to 1972.)

GLENN L. BRUDVIG
Head, Bio-Medical Library
University of Minnesota
Minneapolis, Minnesota

# The Development of a Minicomputer System for the University of Minnesota Bio–medical Library

The University of Minnesota Bio-Medical Library received a three-year grant of $361,729 from the National Library of Medicine in June 1972 to develop a low-cost, stand-alone, library-controlled computer system which would handle book ordering, serials check-in and control, accounting, cataloging, circulation, and reference assistance—a complete, integrated library data management system. The project, as of April 1974, has one year of developmental work before the system becomes fully operational. The design of the system has been completed, but procedures for staff use of the system and display and printing formats are still under development. Part of this paper therefore describes procedures which may be modified before the project is completed.

## Background

The minicomputer system will be based on automated procedures which have been in operation in the Bio-Medical Library for over six years. The first automation program in the library was a serials system which went into operation in January 1968. This system, soon to be replaced, handles all aspects of serials control in a batch processing operation using a CDC 3300 computer. It produces a monthly check-in list of predicted journals, monthly journal holdings lists with daily supplements for staff and patron use, binding slips, and special lists of various kinds.

In July 1969 a second automated system went into operation for acquisitions, again using batch processing and the CDC 3300 computer. The acquisitions system produces periodic lists of all materials in process, including titles requested but not ordered, ordered but not received, received but awaiting cataloging, or cataloged but cards not yet filed. It prints purchase orders and handles accounting operations.

In 1970 procedures for handling the payment history records for serials were added to the automated system so that accounting records for both books and journals could be handled through one operation. These batch procedures have operated very successfully, with few problems, full staff acceptance, economy, and improvement of public services. The minicomputer system is designed to expand automated procedures to all library operations, particularly to circulation and cataloging.

The systems which have been in operation do not have a direct relationship to the design of the minicomputer system since a complete new design is necessary to achieve an integrated system for operation on a minicomputer. The crucial importance of these batch operations to the mini system is in providing a background of experience for library staff, and some of the systems people who worked on them, so that staff members can make meaningful contributions to the development of the mini system. The transition to the mini system should therefore be relatively easy to make in terms of staff acceptance and involvement.

Although none of the software used in the present operations will be used in the mini system, as much of the data as possible will be captured for the new system; some of it, however, may have to be rekeyed or edited. For example, the data in the present serials system are all in upper-case while the mini system will use both upper and lower case. To convert the data we may either convert all records to lower case and edit them to upper case as needed or pull the Bio-Medical Library serials records from the Minnesota Union List of Serials, which has a full ALA character-set. Coded information, holdings statements, payment history information, vendor name and address files, and other data in the serials system will be converted to the new system and some additional information will have to be added.

For the acquisitions system, we may run the old batch operations in parallel with the new on-line system for a period, possibly long enough to let most of the old records pass completely through the ordering process, and manually convert the records at the point of cataloging. Or, we may convert the acquisitions file to the new system at once and edit the records in the cataloging portion of the system; but this is still to be resolved.

We have no cost figures for manual operations to compare costs of the mini system with—only the costs of the present batch systems. We expect significant savings of staff time once the system is fully operational, but have not attempted to predict them. Our present batch processing costs for computer time for serials averages $400 per month for 3,002 current titles, and the acquisitions and accounting operations averages $500 per month. Keypunch rental and punch card costs will be eliminated under the new system and paper supply costs will be considerably reduced. We expect to eliminate as many paper forms as possible and all in-process manual files. The minicomputer system has been purchased and, therefore, the only continuing costs for the system will be for maintennace, which should be only a few hundred dollars per year.

Under the present automated operations we experienced a reduction in both clerical and professional staff needs, but an increase in paraprofessional staff. Clerical positions were upgraded and some duties previously handled by librarians were shifted to paraprofessionals. We expect much the same shift in personnel costs to occur under the mini system. However, most costs benefits will occur in catalog card production and circulation records management.

## Staff

After we received the grant to develop the minicomputer system, the first order of business was to recruit staff. The project staff assembled had a good working knowledge of the Bio-Medical Library operations, a total familiarity with our present systems, and a wide range of experience in systems design. All of the people on the project are part of the library staff.

## Equipment and Space

After the staff was recruited, the selection of the equipment became the next priority. This process is discussed by Grosch elsewhere in this volume. The total cost of equipment purchased for the Bio-Medical Library system will come to about $125,000. The first equipment components were delivered in April 1973 with the second portion in May and June 1973. The first visual terminal was received in December 1973 but the communication equipment needed to connect it to the computer was not installed until March 1974. The delays in getting the equipment have been a constant problem and have slowed the development of the project to a certain degree but not to the point of creating a serious problem. Heavy orders for minicomputers and components have made it difficult for dealers to meet delivery schedules.

The library converted a conference room of 304 sq. ft. into a computer room. Additional wiring and phone outlets were required, but that was the extent of remodeling costs. The area was already air conditioned.

## Acquisitions

Although we have not yet completed the design of the display and print formats, nor the detailed procedures for staff use of the system, I will cover in a general way the procedures which will be followed in processing materials, to present an idea of how the system will work from a librarian's point of view. (The design of the system is covered by Lourey elsewhere in this volume.)

Starting with a request to order a book, the acquisitions assistant will first check the systems files to see if the item has already been requested, ordered, received, or cataloged. (Until such time as the entire card catalog is on-line, we will have to check the card catalog either before or after searching the automated file to avoid possible duplication.) To access the system, the acquisitions assistant enters an identification code on the CRT terminal and indicates which file she wants to see. For a book request she will search the file by either author, title, series, or LC or International Standard Book Number to see if the title is in the file. If she does not find it, she can then proceed to enter the request into the system. Figure 1 shows a screen display for a monograph order. This display and figure 2 illustrate the different data

```
NAME:   Isaacs, Nathan
        1928 -

Title:  (Specify main title 1, additional titles 2) 1. Brief introduction
        to Piaget; the growth of understanding in the young child

Title:   2.  Growth of understanding in the young child
Edition:  2nd ed.
Place:   New York
Publisher:  Agathon Press
Date:   [c1974]
Collation:  121 p.
Notes:  Earlier ed. has title:  The growth of understanding in the young child
Dashed  on Entry:
Notes:
L.C. Subject:
MeSH Subject:  Child psychology
MeSH Subject:  Mental processes - in infancy and childhood
MeSH Subject:  Piaget, Jean, 1896 -
Lib. Status:  R (Req)                               Destination:   B
Verification Source:  NLM
CIP Pub?:  Yes                            Expected date:  9/74
Claim Dates:  1.  _____ to:  _____
              2.  _____      _____
              3.  _____      _____

Requestor's Name and Address:  Dr. Ossey
                               Box 430
                               Mayo

Record Numbers and Order Information:  Order No.  _____
                                       ISSN        0
                                       ISBN 0-87586-029-X
                                       LC 75-168547
                                       Pub. Cat. No.  _____ Item No.  _____
```

**Fig. 1. Screen Display for a Monograph Order**

```
Vendor's Name:  Login

No. Copies:  1              No. of Vols.:

List Price:  $4.95

Order Notes:

Subaccount:  201

Fund:  (specify if other than state)

Donor:

Type of Item:  M
          (M = Mono  S = Ser.  C = Cont.  D = Doc.  DS = Doc. Ser.)

Category:  N
          (N = New book  AC = Added copy  AE = Added edit  AV = Added val.
          R = Replacement)
Payment:  N
          (N = New  SO = St. Ord.  G = Gift  E = Exch.  M = Memb.
          X = Paid as part of other order  DA = Deposit account)

Invoice No.:  34568                          Date:  11/12/74

University No.:  845967

Expenditure:
```

**Fig. 2. A Continuation Screen Display for a Monograph Order**

elements in the book ordering portion of the system. These are not the way the final display formats will look, however, since a series of displays for this information will be used. The acquisitions assistant inputs data into the system by filling in the information, such as name, title, publisher, place, etc., and selecting from a list of data categories, such as type of item, category, or payment.

If the acquisitions assistant has full cataloging information available, she will enter all the information that she has, including a verification source, and will indicate that the status of the record is a request. If the information she has is incomplete, she can enter what she has and collect the rest of the data and add it later. When the record is complete, the acquisitions librarian will call up the record, possibly correct or add information, such as the vendor or fund number, and indicate that the item is ready for order.

On a regular basis, the system would print out purchase orders, either on a purchase order form or possibly in a list by dealer. Initially the purchase orders will be printed on the system's high-speed printer, but eventually we hope to have a slow-speed, remote printer adjacent to the acquisitions terminal so that purchase orders could be printed whenever the librarian wanted them, with rush orders printed on demand. The system would update the accounting records, encumber funds, and adjust financial records whenever orders were generated.

When the book and invoice are received in the library, the record is again called up on the screen and additional information added to it, such as price paid, invoice number, and university number (see figure 3). The invoice is then cleared for payment and the book is ready to go to cataloging.

```
Isaacs, Nathan, 1928
        Brief introduction to Piaget; the growth of understanding in
        the young child.  New York, Agathon Press, c1974.
        0-87586-029-X  75-168547
                        Correct book?  Enter Y or N
Y

Library Status:  Received/approve invoice

List Price:  $4.95

Subaccount:  201

Fund:  State

Type of Item:  Monograph

Category:  New book

Payment Type:  New

Invoice No.:  34565

Date:  11/12/74

University No.:  845967

Expenditure:  $5.50
```

**Fig. 3. Screen Display for Clearing Monograph Order for Payment**

## Cataloging

When the cataloger gets the book, she calls up the same data on the screen to see if the cataloging information is correct but now the acquisitions data is formatted for the cataloger (see figure 4). The data which are missing in the record, for example the size of the book and call number in figure 4, are added and the record is checked for accuracy. Cataloging worksheets would be printed on demand to provide the cataloging staff with a means to collect data from other sources, such as from the card catalog, shelflist, subject authority, LC catalogs, etc. The cataloging assistants would probably do most

```
Personal Name:  Isaacs, Nathan, 1928 -

Title:   1.  Brief introduction to Piaget; the growth of understanding
             in the young child
Title:   2.  Growth of understanding in the young child
Edition:  2nd ed.
Place:  New York
Publisher:  Agathon Press
Date:   [c1974]
Collation:  121 p.
Size:   _____
Notes:  Earlier ed. has title:  The growth of understanding in the
             young child

MeSH Subject:  Child psychology
MeSH Subject:  Mental processes -- in infancy and childhood
MeSH Subject:  Piaget, Jean, 1896 -
Destination:  3
Call No.:  _____

ISBN 0-87586-029-X
LC 75-168547
Language of pub.
Orig. Lang. of pub.
Country of pub.
```

**Fig. 4. Screen Display of a Catalog Record for Data Entry and Editing**

of this work and the cataloger would edit the final cataloging record for accuracy. She would check the final record which would appear in a format similar to figure 5. If the cataloging record was incorrect, the cataloger would add or correct data as required. If the record was correct, or after it was corrected, she would so indicate on the terminal, and a slow-speed, remote printer which would sit beside the cataloger's terminal would print out a complete set of cards in upper and lower case and with all diacritical marks required to meet full ALA cataloging standards.

## Serials

New journal arrivals would be checked in by the serials assistant by calling for a display of a check-in record for the title in hand using a title search key, i.e., the first few letters of the first words in the title.

The serial check-in record would indicate which issues were predicted to arrive, which issues claimed or ordered, and which volumes were at the bindery (see figure 6).

The display format for serials check-in has not yet been designed and would not be the same as illustrated in figure 5, but the data elements would be the same. Figure 5 shows two predicted issues, and one that has been

Final card proof (unit card)

If incorrect request --
   return to cataloging proof
If correct request -- print cards


610.4  Isaacs, Nathan, 1928 -
Is2a      Brief introduction to Piaget;
       the growth of understanding in
       the young child. 2nd. edition.
       New York, Agathon Press [c1974].
       121 p. 23 cm.

          Earlier edition has title:
       The growth of understanding in the
       young child.


1.  Child psychology.  2.  Mental processes -- in infancy and childhood.
3.  Piaget, Jean, 1896 -          Title.
Title:  Growth of understanding in the
young child.

ISBN 0-87586-029-X     75-166547
SRN 0000287


**Fig. 5. Screen Display for a Catalog Card Record
for Proofreading Before Cards are Printed**


American Journal of Diseases of Children

| Ser. | Vol. | Issue | Part | Date | Loc. | Circ. | Cat. | Disp. |
|------|------|-------|------|------|------|-------|------|-------|
|      | 126  | 6     |      | Dec 1973 | CPR-011 | 5 | S | Claim |
|      | 127  | 3     |      | Mar 1974 | CPR-011 | 5 | S |       |
|      | 127  | 4     |      | Apr 1974 | CPR-011 | 5 | S |       |

**Fig. 6. Screen Display for Serials Check-in Record**

claimed. The check-in procedure would consist of entering an abbreviated code for each issue which matches the predicted issue. If a date or issue number were different than predicted, the record could be corrected on the CRT terminal and the prediction of the next issue would be adjusted automatically. When a journal is checked in, the holdings statement for that title would be automatically updated.

## Binding

The system would produce lists of materials ready for binding for the binding assistant to use for collecting journals from the stacks. The binding information and instructions would be displayed in a way similar to figure 7.

| European Journal of Pharmacy | | | | | | | |
|------|------|------------|-------|-----------|------|-------|------|
| Vol. | Date | Title Page | Index | Tab. Cont. | Loc. | Circ. | Disp. |
| 23 | 1973 | First | Last | None | 053 | 5 | Bind |
| 24 | 1973 | First | Last | None | 053 | 5 | Bind |

**Fig. 7. Screen Display for a Serial Binding Record**

If the volume collected for binding was complete, a code would be keyed in on the terminal. The system would then print out binding instructions forms, either upon demand or periodically. The serials holding record would be adjusted to indicate that the particular volume was at the bindery. When the bound volume was returned from the bindery, it would be checked in through the serials check-in procedure in the same manner as a new journal issue arrival. This operation would be very similar to our present bindery operation except that it would use an on-line visual screen rather than printed listings.

## Reference

The reference librarians would be able to search the acquisitions and cataloging files in response to a patron request to see if an item was on order or in process, or if the cataloging had been completed. If necessary, the reference librarian can add the name of the patron to the record so that he would be notified when the book was received and cataloged.

As cataloging records are completed and added to the file, an on-line catalog would be built up which would be searchable by author, title, series, call number, and subject, or in any combination of these elements. Eventually we would hope to convert the records in the card catalog to provide a complete on-line catalog, but this will have to wait until funds are secured.

Serials would probably be the most common record called up at the reference desk. Figure 8 illustrates a display of serials record showing complete holdings, both bound and unbound, indicating that the one issue has been claimed, and which is expected next. Volumes at the bindery would also be displayed in this record. Printed lists for patron use would be run periodically.

American Journal of Diseases of Children

Copy 1.   Bound holdings:   V.1-125 (1911 - Jun 1973)

Unbound holdings:   V. 126 no. 1-5 (Jul 1973 - Nov 1973)

V. 126 no. 6 (Dec 1973) claimed

V. 127 no. 1-3 (Jan 1974 - Mar 1974)

Next expected:   V. 127 no. 4 (Apr 1974)

Location:   Current issue in Current Periodical Room

Stack 011

**Fig. 8. Display of a Serials Record for Reference**

## Circulation

A circulation system will be developed for the mini system, but we will not be able to put it into full operation because we do not have funds for converting back records. We plan to develop the system just the same and use it for the reserve collection until it can be expanded to a full circulation system. The circulation system would use bar-encoded labels which would be affixed to the book or journal and to the borrower's ID card. A book would be checked out by passing a light-sensitive wand reader over the label on the book and the label on the borrower's ID card.

The circulation system is planned to handle overdues, fines, recalling of materials, statistics, and all circulation file management functions. We plan to link the wand reader to a CRT terminal so that records could be displayed, if desired, as materials are checked out. For example, if the borrower had materials overdue this could be displayed on the screen to remind him that they should be returned.

## Potential Future Developments

The project has one more year to go before it becomes operational. The project has opened up many new opportunities for further systems development; one of the most promising is the potential for linking minicomputers together so that one library would be able to gain access to the records of another and vice versa. For example, if a search of the journal file in one library did not locate the title wanted, the system could automatically switch to a sister library, or to another library in a network, to see if it held the title wanted, and so on in a round robin search of linked systems. This problem is beyond the scope of the project, but it illustrates a potential of the minicomputer for regional library networks.

Another potential future development, mentioned above, would be to put the complete card catalog records of the Bio-Medical Library into the system. A preliminary analysis of this problem has been completed and an estimate has been made that it would cost $144,000 to add the 230,000 volumes in the library to the system. These costs would include staff and purchase of additional disks and terminals.

The system also has the potential to maintain a full-scale management information system for the library. If the total library records were in the system, statistics on all library operations could be readily collected, such as circulation statistics by subject category and type of user which could be related to costs of purchasing and servicing materials. This would enable the system to determine the costs for providing service to different kinds of users or for different subject areas. The management system could also help determine where duplicate titles were needed, what parts of the collection needed further development, which titles should be retired to storage or withdrawn, which user groups were putting heavy pressure on the library's resources and which are not. It could also provide information on peak periods of use and provide a variety of data to justify and defend budget requests and allocations.

The minicomputer should reduce costs of library automation to the point where libraries of reasonable size can afford their own system. Both equipment and software, tailored to the particular needs of a library, should be available as a package in the not-too-distant future so that a library could purchase a complete system and avoid expensive developmental costs.

EUGENE D. LOUREY
Research Associate
Bio-Medical Library Mini-Computer Project
University of Minnesota
Minneapolis, Minnesota

# Systems Design for a Minicomputer-Based Library Data Management System

In the past, most automated systems employed large, general purpose processors, or very specialized applications software, usually both. An approach employing either method does not support library automation in any but the largest and best-financed libraries. Smaller libraries must either affiliate with these larger libraries or share equipment with nonlibrary applications. In either case, processing methodologies, standards and equipment decisions are made outside the affected library by persons unfamiliar with their requirements.

Current technology and pricing make this approach to library automation unnecessarily restrictive to individual libraries and unnecessarily expensive for the library community. Equipment selected for its suitability in library-type problems combined with generalized data management software designed for library applications will make dedicated, self-contained systems cost effective for most libraries.

## THE SYSTEM

At the University of Minnesota Bio-Medical Library, we are building an automated library data management system. The system will encompass all aspects of library processing activities: acquisitions, serials, cataloging, circulation, and reference services. It is an on-line, integrated system built to be a prototype which can easily be exported to other libraries. It is based upon low-cost, dedicated minicomputer hardware and advanced software concepts.

## Hardware

For our system we have selected hardware which we believe is particularly well suited to library applications. Our CPU is a DEC PDP 11/40. This is a 16-bit machine with excellent character processing capability. It is very fast, is memory-expandable to 256K bytes, and has memory management which is comparable to virtual memory and memory protect. Also, peripheral attachment options are unlimited. This is important for libraries since some peripherals devices which will be very useful for them are not yet perfected.

We are using removable pack disks as our on-line storage devices. We presently have a single controller and a single 40 million character drive. Both are marketed and maintained by DEC. We can attach up to 8 drives to a controller and multiple controllers to the CPU. This is an area where we are expecting price and technology changes. Prices have been falling steadily for several years and libraries are ideal applications for read-only storage devices which have a high potential for cheap, permanent on-line storage.

We have two industry compatible 9-channel 800 BPI tape drives. The first is for transaction recording; the second is for off-line sequential storage, exchanging data with other systems, and back-up for the transaction recording unit.

Our central printer is a high-speed 132-column line printer. We expect to use this capability only for the production of long hard copy lists and for problem diagnosis memory dumps. We plan to have operational print capabilities decentralized to provide system users direct control over the preparation of such materials as orders, claims, cancellations, cataloging worksheets, catalog cards, fine notices, recalls, and bibliographies. This decentralized print capability will consist of selectable font printer/plotters with independent horizontal and vertical carriage control. These devices can satisfy virtually any hard copy print requirements but are low-speed and thus relatively inexpensive.

Our user terminals are Superbee CRT and keyboard terminals. These devices are excellent for data entry. They have character and line editing capabilities, 2048 characters of terminal memory, a large screen size (25 by 80 characters), and a large number of displayable characters. Their screen size and memory capacity also make them excellent for file inquiry.

These devices, with the exception of the low-speed printers, are already installed and in use for test purposes. We expect to acquire two additional devices, both primarily for circulation: a wand reader for identification of library materials and borrowers, and a special printer for preparation of labels with bar coding to support the wand reader.

## Software

The software for our system employs several techniques to minimize development time, development effort, and core requirements, and to maximize system flexibility—modularity, runtime parameters, dictionary descriptions of data items, assembly time parameters, and control by user command. These techniques are not new, but the use of them all in one system, the use of them in library systems, and the use of them with minicomputers is quite uncommon.

Our software is designed and programmed in small self-contained modules. Each module performs a specific activity but is generalized so that it can perform its activity in a variety of circumstances. An example of such a generalized module is the table conversion routine. It searches a user-specified table which it reads from disk storage for an equivalent argument and returns the conversion value. The lengths of the table, argument, and conversion value are all variables. These small modules are easier to debug, easier to change if necessary, and they reduce total system core requirements.

Modules are particularly important for those areas of the system which are common to all applications such as searching indexes, extracting field values from a record for output generation, and converting encoded data to display form. They are also important for software interfacing with peripheral devices. Input and output from all devices will be converted to our internal form. Only the interface software will deal with data in its external form. In this way, adding new peripherals will only require adding a new external interface module to the system repertoire of software modules. Also, interfacing with another system will only require adding a software interface to make the exchange data compatible.

Runtime parameters control the execution of all modules. Requests for execution of any module require specifications of the values of the module variables. For example, a request to execute the table conversion routine includes specification of the table to be used, the length and address of the argument and the length and address of the output buffer. The parameterization of these modules reduces the number of modules and the amount of core required at the expense of execution time. For our application this is a very good tradeoff, since execution time is essentially free in a dedicated system which is I/O bound.

Dictionary descriptions control all data entry, all accesses to the data base, and all output generation. Every file, record, field, index, and I/O format is described in a dictionary. Each module which accesses the data base, interprets input, or prepares output uses these dictionary descriptions. For example, the table (file) used in the table conversion routine is described in a dictionary which indicates its length, its address, its ordering scheme, and the records it contains. Each record in this case contains a pair of values, the argument, and the result of the conversion, which are also described in dictionaries. Use of these dictionaries makes all software independent of the data base. Changes to the data base will not require any modification of the software.

Assembly time parameters are used for all program references to the dictionary and to all system-defined values and references. This permits changes to the format and contents of the dictionary and restructuring of core with no changes in existing software. For instance, if a new variable is added to the description of files to accommodate a file which is treated differently than others in one or more modules, a modification of the affected modules and a reassembly of others which access the file dictionary will permit the addition of the new variable anywhere in the dictionary format. Or, if the locations in core of system defined values—such as date and clock time—are changed, a reassembly of the system will accomplish the change.

User commands control the operation of all components of the system except file security, file back-up, and management statistics. In general this is true of all interactive systems, but our software architecture provides a whole new dimension to user command control of system operation. As a result of our use of small generalized modules rather than comprehensive applications programs, users can schedule a sequence of events, with appropriate parameters for each, in much more detail. This gives users a greater opportunity to make the system responsive to their needs. At the same time, users are not required to specify all actions in great detail; default conditions will be operative when not overridden by user specification.

As an example, consider a request for an author index search. If nothing is specified except the author entry, the system will assume: that the user wants to inspect all cross references, that the output format is standard, and that the output medium is the CRT terminal device. However, if the user desired, he could specify the cross references to be shown, specify the categories of author entries to be shown, specify that subject classifications are desired in addition to the standard output, and specify that a hard copy list in order by title is required. In fact, the user can specify any combination of values of the variables he may desire.

We have devoted considerable time and effort to making this system exportable. This has required close attention to two aspects of the system: cost and versatility. An exportable system must be cost effective in many environments and it must be versatile enough to meet many differing processing requirements. There are many aspects to both cost and versatility which influenced our design and implementation decisions.

## Cost Considerations

Total system costs include costs of hardware, hardware maintenance, site preparation, installation, operations, software maintenance, and supplies. During this project our principal cost emphasis has been to keep all these elements of cost to a minimum for subsequent installations of the system rather than for the project. Thus we have put extra software effort into making the system flexible, and we have purchased and are purchasing equipment which will be operational for subsequent applications of the system.

### HARDWARE

The purchase price of minicomputers is considerably below that of larger processors. But there are other factors which make our approach significantly less expensive. Our modular software design is ideally suited to the hardware modularity of minicomputer architecture. All system hardware can be purchased as needed. The user pays for only what is actually needed and only when it is needed. Any peripheral device can be attached to our system; thus the least expensive device which meets the requirements can be acquired. Since DEC is by far the largest manufacturer of minicomputers, hardware interfaces between peripheral devices and DEC CPUs are usually available when the device is introduced or shortly thereafter. DEC users are seldom required to have these interfaces specially built for their use. Our use of generalized common modules in software implementation keeps core requirements to a minimum. Furthermore, the system executive has memory swapping capability enabling much of the system to be resident on the disk and only pulled into core when needed. All of these factors make the hardware costs of our approach minimal in comparison with any other.

### HARDWARE MAINTENANCE

Low-cost hardware will also be less expensive to maintain, since there is usually a direct relationship between total system hardware costs and hardware maintenance costs. Furthermore, minicomputers are structurally and operationally simpler in design and require a great deal less maintenance than large, general purpose systems. Whereas large systems generally have between 10 and 20 hours of regularly scheduled preventative maintenance per week, minicomputer installations require no regularly scheduled preventative maintenance. Mean time to failure on mini systems is measured in months rather than hours. The dependability of minis is explained by their development background. They were created primarily for the military and aerospace markets to operate in spacecraft, in ships, and in mobile land vehicles. The durability of these early minis has been a benchmark for later developments.

## SITE PREPARATION

Site preparation for minicomputers is relatively uninvolved in comparison to the major modifications required for large systems. Minis are physically smaller and take less room. They generate less heat and have higher tolerance for adverse conditions, high or low temperature and humidity. They do not require raised floors, special air conditioning or water cooling. Generally they will operate in completely unmodified surroundings. In addition, we are decentralizing operations by attaching remote peripheral devices which require no site preparation except clearing the space and dropping the lines to the remote sites. This reduces space and electrical requirements at the central site.

## INSTALLATION

Because the hardware is architecturally simple and reliable, hardware installation and acceptance testing require little staff time. Our software approach will hopefully make software installation equally problem-free. Our methods require less code, result in more thoroughly tested code, enable most changes to be made without any recoding, and enable software changes where required to be made without unforeseen consequences. With good documentation and training materials, the cost of installation of this system should be well below any system of comparable capability.

## OPERATIONS

System printing functions are decentralized so no operations staff are required to monitor and oversee the printing activities. System files are all on-line so tape loading and disk mounting of data files will not be required. Errors encountered during system operation can be reported to terminal operators for notification of maintenance staff, so central site monitoring for system failures will be unnecessary. Except for analysis and correction of system failures, no EDP-skilled personnel will be required for system operations. Any tape mounting, disk pack mounting, printer ribbon changing, or paper loading which may occasionally be required can be done by anyone with a few hours of training.

## SOFTWARE MAINTENANCE

Less code and more thoroughly debugged code will obviously result in lower maintenance costs. Furthermore, all systems which are installed will be able to communicate with each other, making it possible for maintenance staff from a single site to implement corrections or modifications from any site to all other sites. Any modification to a system which is developed to accommodate any new device or any unique processing requirement will be available, once developed, to all other systems using the same software; and these modifications can be incorporated from any system to any other as the need arises.

## SUPPLY COSTS

Since all system files are on-line and available on demand from any system entry point, no hard copy materials will be required for daily operations. Adequate backup will eliminate the need for hard copy data for recovery in the event of catastrophic failure. Where hard copies are needed for orders, claims, overdue notices, etc., the number of copies required can be kept to just the number sent out. No copies for the library need be kept since they can be recreated when needed. The decentralized printers can produce any required form. This will minimize the need for expensive preprinted forms.

## Versatility

An exportable system must be able to accommodate changing requirements within a library over time, and different requirements in different libraries. The most important system variables which must be dealt with are: data base size; data base contents; data base structure; staffing, organizational, and processing patterns; number of processing stations or system entry points; volume of activity; data entry and output requirements; network participation; and new hardware technology.

### DATA BASE SIZE

Minicomputer hardware can be configured to maintain any amount of data in the data base. On-line storage can be added as needed with no limit. However, if more than 1 billion characters are needed, it might be desirable to add another processor. The size of the data base could only affect the software if a different device were added to increase the on-line storage capacity. In this case, the only change would be a software interface module to handle the new device.

## DATA BASE CONTENT

Our software makes no assumptions about the content of the data base; it is entirely defined by the data base dictionary. The content of the data base can be established initially to meet requirements as of that time. Later, it can be changed if the requirements change. For instance, if initially a library does not enter and maintain the physical dimensions of materials, but later decides these items should be included in the data base, the system can modify the file to provide for this data, print a worklist of items for which these values are not completed, and display upon demand records requiring completion of these values so the values can be entered. If the initial decision was to include this data, but later it is found to be unnecessary, the system can modify the data base to eliminate these values.

## DATA BASE STRUCTURE

Our data management system includes extensive interfile and intrafile cross reference capability. This provides for as many inverted file indexes as are necessary. It also provides for all library type cross references: see, see also, see from, see also from, etc. In addition, every field can be defined as variable length and as having a variable number of values in a record. Furthermore, every file can have any number of uniquely defined records. These features make the structure of the users data base entirely variable in our system.

## STAFFING, ORGANIZATIONAL, AND PROCESSING PATTERNS

The system contains a very flexible data base security system. Limits upon use can be based on particular user, class of user, terminal in use, type of data, source of data or any combination of these factors. Further, use can be subdivided into data entry, validation, modification, or examination with security restrictions applying differently to each. Security options are established at installation time, although they can be redefined later if that becomes necessary. It is up to the system users in each operating environment to establish who can perform which functions on what data from which terminal sites. Thus, the system can accommodate any breakdown of tasks, responsibilities, and authorities.

## NUMBER OF PROCESSING STATIONS OR SYSTEM ENTRY POINTS

As with most interactive applications systems, the number of terminals serviced is not a critical factor for the software. Applications software is identical for one terminal as for hundreds. Systems software may be affected by a large number of terminals, but our systems software is designed assuming a variable number of terminals. The only constraint on the number of terminals attached to our system is the cost of the hardware. As the number of terminals attached increases, it may be necessary to add multiplexers, concentrators, or even additional processors. None of these will require any modification of the software.

## VOLUME OF ACTIVITY

Activity volume has implications for the hardware, but does not affect system software. If high volumes are creating a CPU bottleneck, causing unacceptable response times, more core or a parallel CPU can be added at minimal cost (under $10,000). If on-line storage access is overtaxed by high volumes, additional controllers or serial processors can be added. If high volumes are creating terminal communication bottlenecks, higher speed circuits could be installed, or multiplexers, concentrators, or serial processors could be added. None of these hardware expansions would require any software modification.

## DATA ENTRY AND OUTPUT REQUIREMENTS

Input and output formats and contents are user defined within broad limits. However, it is impossible to develop generalized software for data entry and output preparation which will provide for all possible forms of data exchange. Even if it were possible, the overhead would be too high to make it feasible. Our system can interpret input and prepare output for all local purposes, but software interface modules will be required for many external communications activities. For instance, our software would not be able to accept as input or prepare as output a magnetic tape for photo composition without a special module for this purpose. Similarly, it might not be able to communicate directly with other automated systems without a specially built software interface for formatting output and reformatting input.

Another form of output which the user can define within limits but cannot completely control without software modification is management reporting. Exception reporting with variable limits will be used to notify system users of a potential problem: an acquisitions account being expended too quickly; a user with many materials borrowed and overdue attempting to borrow more materials; or a consistent variation between estimated price for a class of materials and their actual price—a variation great enough to affect long-range budget planning. However, if observation of different factors than those provided is desired, program modifications will be required. Establishment of control limits for exception reporting entails sufficient system overhead that we will only provide those currently thought to be desirable.

## NETWORK PARTICIPATION

Hardware interfaces are either already available or can be developed at reasonable cost to attach any on-line systems together. With the addition of the necessary hardware and perhaps a special purpose software module, our system can be attached to any other system with no changes required on the other end. This link can be to give them access to our data base, to give us access to theirs, or to do both. Thus our system can serve as a self-contained node in a large network of libraries, as a central source for a network of users, or in both capacities simultaneously for different purposes.

## NEW HARDWARE TECHNOLOGY

As previously mentioned, the inclusion in the system of any new (to the system or to the market) peripheral device creates no difficult problems. In some cases, a software interface module will be required for intercepting and translating input and output, but these are inexpensive to develop once the characteristics of the new device are known. However, if it becomes desirable to use a different CPU, it will be necessary to recode but not to redesign the system unless a symbolic code conversion package or a hardware PDP 11/40 emulator is available for the new processor.

It should be clear that our system, in concept and implementation, is quite unlike previous library automation systems. We employ very inexpensive hardware, only that which is actually required to do the job at hand, and software tailor-made for library applications, but general enough to serve the needs of a wide variety of library environments. The project was proposed and funded as a prototype readily exportable to other libraries. We are still more than a year away from project completion, but are increasingly confident that our system will be able to fulfill that promise.

We expect our approach to make automation technology available to libraries with very modest resources and budgets. Furthermore, these individual libraries will be able to tailor their system to serve their particular needs, as they define them.

# INDEX

Application programs, 16, 114.

BALLOTS System (Stanford University), description, 80-82; PDP 11 mini-computer, 82-84; programmable terminals, 85-87, 89-90; proposed circulation system, 91-93.

Batch systems, 11-12; at the University of Maryland, 34-38; in information retrieval, 97-98; to update files, 48.

Bibliographic networks, 136.

BIBNET (Information Dynamics Corp.), access to other data bases, 154; data base, 140-42; interlibrary communication, 154-55; network design objectives, 138-39; reasons for using minicomputers, 136; purposes, 138, 156-57; use for cataloging, 142-52.

CHASM (Chicago Access Support Module), 112, 114.

Choosing a minicomputer system, 93-94, 165-67; at the University of Chicago, 115-17.

Circulation systems, automated, at the University of Maryland, 34-38; BALLOTS proposed system, 91-93; LIBS 100 System, 54-75.

Computer output onto microfilm- produced catalogs, 154.

Cost benefits of minicomputers, 171-72, 180, 185-88; at the University of Maryland, 40; at the University of Pennsylvania, 48.

Data processing in library education, 122-24; as a learning experience, 133, 135.

Electronics expertise, need for, 117, 119.

Files, access to, 112, 114; construction of, 108-12; in BALLOTS System, 81-82, 91; maintenance, 60-65, 81-82.

Front end configuration, at the University of Chicago, 114-15; at the University of Maryland, 36ff.; at Stanford University, 82-85; description, 14-17; in information retrieval, 98-99.